Syntactic Theory

CSLI Lecture Notes
Number 92

Syntactic Theory

A Formal Introduction

Ivan A. Sag & Thomas Wasow

CSLI
PUBLICATIONS
Center for the Study of
Language and Information
Stanford, California

Copyright © 1999
CSLI Publications
Center for the Study of Language and Information
Leland Stanford Junior University
Printed in the United States
03 02 01 00 99   5 4 3 2 1

Library of Congress Cataloging-in-Publication Data

Sag, Ivan A., 1949–
Syntactic theory : a formal introduction / Ivan A. Sag & Tom Wasow.
p.   cm. – (CSLI lecture notes ; no. 92)
Includes bibliographical references (p.) and index.
ISBN 1-57586-161-5 (alk. paper).
ISBN 1-57586-160-7 (pbk. : alk. paper)
1. Grammar, Comparative and general–Syntax. I. Wasow, Thomas. II. Title.
III. Series.
P291.S25   1999
415—dc21   98-52509
CIP

∞ The acid-free paper used in this book meets the minimum requirements of
the American National Standard for Information Sciences—Permanence of
Paper for Printed Library Materials, ANSI Z39.48-1984.

CSLI was founded early in 1983 by researchers from Stanford University, SRI
International, and Xerox PARC to further research and development of integrated
theories of language, information, and computation. CSLI headquarters and CSLI
Publications are located on the campus of Stanford University.

CSLI Publications reports new developments in the study of language, information,
and computation. In addition to lecture notes, our publications include
monographs, working papers, revised dissertations, and conference proceedings.
Our aim is to make new results, ideas, and approaches available as quickly as
possible. Please visit our web site at
http://csli-publications.stanford.edu/
for comments on this and other titles, as well as for changes and corrections by the
author and publisher.

In memory of our fathers

William E. Sag (1908–1977)

Wolfgang R. Wasow (1909–1993)

Contents

Preface

This textbook grew out of our efforts to develop teaching material for the undergraduate-level Introduction to Syntax course that has been taught at Stanford University for over twenty years. We used earlier versions of this text for three years; the final version was revised and expanded many times to satisfy the needs of our students, whose feedback has been of immense value in shaping the present volume. We consider ourselves fortunate to have extremely talented and demanding students, whose influence shines through our prose on every page.

In addition, more than one colleague has used our text successfully in first-year graduate classes. We feel it is particularly well suited to general readers or those who work in disciplines related to linguistics, such as psychology, philosophy, mathematics, or computer science. All that is required is an interest in rigorous approaches to the analysis of the grammatical structure of natural languages.

We have tried to strike a balance between linguistic analysis (centered on the development of increasingly broader grammar fragments) and data-oriented problem solving. In addition, we have tried to place the proposals presented here into historical perspective (Chapter 1 and Appendix B). A Glossary is included both to aid the reader unfamiliar with traditional grammatical terminology and to provide easy access to more technical jargon that we have employed.

Chapters 1 through 8 develop most of the technical machinery used in the rest of the book. This section of the text is self-contained and can be used as the basis of an abbreviated introductory course. Chapter 9 contains a summary of the grammar develped in Chapters 1 through 8, along with some general discussion of language processing by humans and computers.

Chapters 10 through 13 apply the tools developed in the earlier chapters to some well-studied grammatical phenomena. Chapter 14 introduces a topic not normally included in theoretical syntax courses, namely language variation. Chapter 15 deals with the basics of the complex topic of long-distance dependencies, and in the process introduces some new analytic devices. Chapter 16 has a special status, introducing a streamlined reformulation of the overall theory in terms of an architecture based on 'signs', not rules. Appendix A summarizes the grammar of English developed in Chapters 1–13 and 15 (but includes neither the material on the dialects discussed in Chapter 14, nor the innovations proposed in Chapter 16).

We have many people to thank for their part in helping us bring this book to completion. First and foremost, we would like to thank three people: Emily Bender (who, as a course assistant and close colleague, commented on many drafts and made contributions throughout the text), Georgia Green (whose painstakingly detailed and helpful comments emerged from her experiences using our text at the University of Illinois at Urbana-Champaign), and Bob Carpenter (whose detailed comments on a near-final draft led us to overhaul the 'squiggly bits', as one of our British colleagues likes to put it). Others who gave us detailed comments on earlier drafts are: Gertraud Benke, Frank van Eynde, Daffyd Gibbon, Adam Przepiorkowski, and Gregory Stump. Frank, Daffyd, and Greg also gave us the benefit of their experiences using our text in their own classes. Special thanks are also due to Dick Hudson and Paul Kay for their help with Appendix B. Others who helped us one way or the other are: Farrell Ackerman, Louise Auerhahn, John Baugh, Renee Blake, Bob Borsley, Amy Brynolfson, Chris Callison-Burch, Myong-hi Chai, Brady Clark, Ann Copestake, Erica Denham, Colin Drake, Penny Eckert, Dan Flickinger, Ryan Ginstrom, Mark Goldenson, Lisa Green, Scott Guffey, Matt Kodoma, Jean-Pierre Koenig, Zakiyyah Langford, Chungmin Lee, Hanjung Lee, Rob Malouf, Michael McDaid, Brian Milch, Toshiaki Nishihara, Susanne Riehemann, Dave McKercher, John Rickford, Rachel Nordlinger, Paul Postal, Geoffrey Pullum, Scott Schwenter, Peter Sells, Stuart Tannock, Shiao Wei Tham, Ida Toivonen, Judith Tonhauser, Louise Vigeant, Rick Warren, and Gert Webelhuth. We would also like to thank Dikran Karagueuzian, Director of CSLI Publications, for his multi-facetted support and patience, as well as Tony Gee and Maureen Burke for their help in matters of production. We also acknowledge the support of an Irvine Multicultural Curriculum grant to Stanford University.

This book was written at Stanford's Center for the Study of Language and Information – an ideal environment for thought and writing. Thanks to John Perry for keeping CSLI a perfect work environment and to Emma Pease for keeping the computers humming. Some of the material in this text is based on research conducted in part under the auspices of CSLI's LINGuistic Grammars Online (LINGO) project. In that connection, we gratefully acknowledge support from the Bundesministerium für Bildung, Wissenschaft, Forschung, und Technologie (BMBF), who support LINGO's participation in the VERBMOBIL project under Grant FKZ:01IV7024.

1

Introduction

1.1   Two Conceptions of Grammar

The reader may wonder, why would a college offer courses on grammar –
a topic that is usually thought of as part of junior high school curriculum
(or even GRAMMAR school curriculum)? Well, the topic of this book is
not the same thing that most people probably think of as grammar.

What is taught as grammar in primary and secondary school is what
linguists call 'prescriptive grammar'. It consists of admonitions not to
use certain forms or constructions that are common in everyday speech.
A prescriptive grammar might contain rules like:

Be sure to never split an infinitive.

Prepositions are bad to end sentences with.

As modern linguists we think that prescriptive grammar is for the
most part a pointless activity. We view human language as a phenomenon amenable to scientific investigation, rather than something to
be regulated by the decrees of authorities. Your seventh grade math
teacher might have discussed the time the Indiana legislature almost
passed a bill establishing the value of π as 3, and everybody in class no
doubt laughed at such foolishness. Linguists regard prescriptive grammar as silly in much the same way: Natural phenomena simply cannot
be legislated.

Of course, we do not deny the existence of powerful social and economic reasons for learning the grammatical norms of educated people.[1]
How these norms get established and their influence on the evolution
of languages are fascinating questions in sociolinguistics and historical
linguistics, but they are beyond the scope of this book. Similarly, we will

---

[1]By the same token, there may well be good economic reasons for standardizing a
decimal approximation to π (though 3 is almost certainly far too crude an approximation for most purposes).

not address issues of educational policy, except to say that in dismissing traditional (prescriptive) grammar instruction, we are not denying that attention to linguistic structure in the classroom can turn students into more effective speakers and writers. Indeed, we would welcome more enlightened grammar instruction in the schools. See Nunberg (1983) for an insightful discussion of these issues.

So, if modern grammarians don't worry about split infinitives and the like, then what do they study? It turns out that human languages are amazingly complex systems, whose inner workings can be investigated in large part simply by consulting the intuitions of native speakers. Here are some examples from English.

Example 1 The adjectives *unlikely* and *improbable* are virtually synonymous: we talk about unlikely or improbable events or heroes, and we can paraphrase *It is improbable that Lee will be elected* by saying *It is unlikely that Lee will be elected.* This last sentence is synonymous with *Lee is unlikely to be elected.* So why does it sound so strange to say **Lee is improbable to be elected?* (In keeping with standard linguistic practice, we will use an asterisk to mark an expression that is not well formed – that is, that doesn't 'sound good' to our ears.)

Example 2 The sentences *They saw Pat with Chris* and *They saw Pat and Chris* are near paraphrases. But if you didn't catch the second name, it would be far more natural to ask *Who did they see Pat with?* than it would be to ask **Who did they see Pat and?* Why do these two nearly identical sentences differ with respect to how we can question their parts? Notice, by the way, that the question that sounds well formed (or 'grammatical' in the linguist's sense) is the one that violates a standard prescriptive rule. The other sentence is so blatantly deviant that prescriptivists would never think to comment on the impossibility of such sentences. Prescriptive rules typically arise because human language use is innovative, leading languages to change. If people never use a particular construction – like the bad example above – there's no point in bothering to make up a prescriptive rule to tell people not to use it.

Example 3 The two sentences *Something disgusting has slept in this bed* and *Something disgusting has happened in this bed* appear on the surface to be grammatically completely parallel. So why is it that the first has a passive counterpart: *This bed has been slept in by something disgusting,* whereas the second doesn't: **This bed has been happened in by something disgusting?*

These are the sorts of questions contemporary grammarians try to answer. The first two will eventually be addressed in this text, but the third will not.[2] The point of introducing them here is to illustrate a fundamental fact that underlies all modern work in theoretical syntax:

> Every normal speaker of any natural language has acquired an immensely rich and systematic body of unconscious knowledge, which can be investigated by consulting speakers' intuitive judgments.

In other words, knowing a language involves mastering an intricate system full of surprising regularities and idiosyncrasies. Languages are phenomena of considerable complexity, which can be studied scientifically. That is, we can formulate general hypotheses about linguistic structure and test them against the facts of particular languages.

The study of grammar on this conception is a field in which hypothesis-testing is particularly easy: the linguist can simply ask native speakers whether the predictions regarding well formedness of crucial sentences are correct.[3] The term 'syntax' is often used instead of 'grammar' in technical work in linguistics. While the two terms are sometimes interchangeable, 'grammar' may also be used more broadly to cover all aspects of language structure; 'syntax', in contrast, refers only to the ways in which words combine into phrases, and phrases into sentences – the form or structure of well formed expressions. Although the boundaries are not sharp, 'syntax' contrasts with 'semantics' (the study of linguistic meaning), 'morphology' (the study of word structure), and 'phonology' (the study of the sound patterns of language) in ways that 'grammar' does not.

⚠ *This symbol before a problem indicates that it should not be skipped. The problem involves something that will either be elaborated upon or else simply incorporated into subsequent chapters.*

---

[2]For extensive discussion of the third question, see Postal (1986).

[3]This methodology is not without its pitfalls. Judgments of acceptability show considerable variation across speakers. Moreover, they can be heavily influenced by context, both linguistic and nonlinguistic. Since linguists rarely make any effort to control for such effects, not all of the data employed in the syntax literature should be accepted without question. On the other hand, many judgments are so unequivocal that they can clearly be relied on. In more delicate cases, many linguists have begun to supplement judgments with data from actual usage, by examining grammatical patterns found in written and spoken corpora. The use of multiple sources and types of evidence is always a good idea in empirical investigations. See Schütze (1996) for a detailed discussion of methodological issues surrounding the use of judgment data in syntactic research.

⚠ **Problem 1: Judging Examples**

Indicate whether each of the following examples is acceptable or unacceptable. If it is unacceptable, give an intuitive explanation of what is wrong with it, i.e. whether it:

a. fails to conform to the rules of English grammar,

b. is grammatically well-formed, but bizarre in meaning (if so, explain why), or

c. contains a feature of grammar that occurs only in a particular variety of English, for example, slang, or a regional dialect; if so, identify the feature. Is it stigmatized in comparison with 'standard' English?

If you are uncertain about any judgments, feel free to consult with others. Nonnative speakers of English, in particular, are encouraged to compare their judgments with others.

  (i) Kim and Sandy is looking for a new bicycle.
 (ii) Have you the time?
(iii) I've never put the book.
 (iv) The boat floated down the river sank.
  (v) It ain't nobody goin to miss nobody.
 (vi) Terry really likes they.
(vii) Chris must liking syntax.
(viii) Aren't I invited to the party?
 (ix) They wondered what each other would do.
  (x) There is eager to be fifty students in this class.
 (xi) They persuaded me to defend themselves.
(xii) Strings have been pulled many times to get people into Harvard.
(xiii) This is the kind of problem that my doctor is easy to talk to about.
(xiv) A long list of everyone's indiscretions were published in the newspaper.
 (xv) Which chemical did you mix the hydrogen peroxide and?
(xvi) There seem to be a good feeling developing among the students.

1.2   An Extended Example

To get a feel for the sort of research syntacticians conduct, consider the following question:

In which linguistic environments do English speakers normally use reflexive pronouns (i.e. forms like *herself* or *ourselves*), and where does it sound better to use a nonreflexive pronoun (e.g. *her, she, us,* or *we*)?

To see how to approach an answer to this question, consider, first, some basic examples:

(1) a. *We like us.
  b. We like ourselves.
  c. She likes her. [where, she ≠ her]
  d. She likes herself.
  e. Nobody likes us.
  f. *Nobody likes ourselves.
  g. *Ourselves like us.
  h. *Ourselves like ourselves.

These examples suggest a generalization along the following lines:

Hypothesis I: *A reflexive pronoun can appear in a sentence only if that sentence also contains a preceding expression that has the same reference (i.e. a preceding* COREFERENTIAL *expression); a nonreflexive pronoun cannot appear in a sentence that contains such an expression.*

The following examples are different from the previous ones in various ways, so they provide a first test of our hypothesis:

(2) a. She voted for her. [she ≠ her]
  b. She voted for herself.
  c. We voted for her.
  d. *We voted for herself.
  e. *We gave us presents.
  f. We gave ourselves presents.
  g. *We gave presents to us.
  h. We gave presents to ourselves.
  i. *We gave us to the cause.
  j. We gave ourselves to the cause.
  k. *Nobody told us about us.
  l. Nobody told us about ourselves.
  m. *Nobody told ourselves about us.
  n. *Nobody told ourselves about ourselves.

These examples are all predicted by Hypothesis I, lending it some initial plausibility. But here are some counterexamples:

(3) a. We think that nobody likes us.
  b. *We think that nobody likes ourselves.

According to our hypothesis, our judgments in (3a,b) should be reversed. Intuitively, the difference between these examples and the earlier ones is that the sentences in (3) contain subordinate clauses, whereas (2) and (1) contain only simple sentences.

Problem 2: Applying Hypothesis I

But it isn't actually the mere presence of the subordinate clauses in (3) that makes the difference. To see why, consider the following, which contain subordinate clauses but are covered by Hypothesis I.

   (i) We think that she voted for her. [she $\neq$ her]
  (ii) We think that she voted for herself.
 (iii)*We think that herself voted for her.
 (iv)*We think that herself voted for herself.

   a. Explain how Hypothesis I accounts for the data in (i)-(iv).
   b. What is it about the subordinate clauses in (3) that makes them different from those in (i)-(iv) with respect to Hypothesis I?

Given our investigation so far, then, we might revise Hypothesis I to the following:

Hypothesis II: *A reflexive pronoun can appear in a clause only if that clause also contains a preceding, coreferential expression; a nonreflexive pronoun cannot appear in any clause that contains such an expression.*

For sentences with only one clause (such as (1)-(2)), Hypothesis II makes the same predictions as Hypothesis I. But it correctly permits (3a) because *we* and *us* are in different clauses, and it rules out (3b) because *we* and *ourselves* are in different clauses.

However, Hypothesis II as stated won't work either:

(4) a. Our friends like us.
     b. *Our friends like ourselves.
     c. Those pictures of us offended us.
     d. *Those pictures of us offended ourselves.
     e. We found a letter to us in the trash.
     f. *We found a letter to ourselves in the trash.

What's going on here? The acceptable examples of reflexive pronouns have been cases (i) where the reflexive pronoun is functioning as an object of a verb (or the object of a preposition that goes with the verb) and (ii) where the antecedent – that is, the expression it is coreferential with – is the subject or a preceding object of the same verb. If we think of a verb as denoting some sort of action or state, then the subject and objects (or prepositional objects) normally denote the participants in that action or state. These are often referred to as the ARGUMENTS of the verb. In the examples in (4), unlike many of the earlier examples, the reflexive pronouns and their antecedents are not arguments of the same verb (or, in other words, they are not COARGUMENTS). For example in (4b), *our* is just part of the subject of the verb *like*, and hence not itself an argument of the verb; rather, it is *our friends* that denotes participants in the liking relation. Similarly, in (4e) the arguments of *found* are *we* and *a letter to us*; *us* is only part of an argument of *found*.

So to account for these differences, we can consider the following:

Hypothesis III: *A reflexive pronoun must be an argument of a verb that has another preceding argument with the same reference. A nonreflexive pronoun cannot appear as an argument of a verb that has a preceding coreferential argument.*

Each of the examples in (4) contains two coreferential expressions (*we, us, our,* or *ourselves*), but none of them contains two coreferential expressions that are arguments of the same verb. Hypothesis III correctly rules out just those sentences in (4) in which the second of the two coreferential expressions is the reflexive pronoun *ourselves*.

Now consider the following cases:

(5)   a.   Vote for us!
     b.   *Vote for ourselves!
     c.   *Vote for you!
     d.   Vote for yourself!

In (5d), for the first time, we find a well formed reflexive with no antecedent. If we don't want to append an *ad hoc* codicil to Hypothesis III,[4] we will need to posit a hidden subject (namely, *you*) in imperative sentences.

Similar arguments can be made with respect to the following sentences.

(6)   a.   We appealed to him$_1$ to vote for him$_2$. [him$_1 \neq$ him$_2$]
     b.   We appealed to him to vote for himself.
     c.   We appealed to him to vote for us.

(7)   a.   We appeared to him to vote for him.

---

[4]For example, an extra clause that says: 'unless the sentence is imperative, in which case a second person reflexive is well formed and a second person nonreflexive pronoun is not.' This would rule out the offending case but not in any illuminating way that would generalize to other cases.

    b. *We appeared to him to vote for himself.

    c. We appeared to him to vote for ourselves.

In (6), the pronouns indicate that *him* is functioning as the subject of *vote*, but it looks like it is the object of the preposition *to*, not an argument of *vote*. Likewise, in (7), the pronouns suggest that *we* should be analyzed as an argument of *vote*, but its position suggests that it is an argument of *appeared*. So, on the face of it, such examples are problematical for Hypothesis III, unless we posit arguments that are in some sense missing. We will return to the analysis of such cases in later chapters.

⚠ Problem 3: Reciprocals

English has a 'reciprocal' expression *each other* (think of it as a single word for present purposes), which behaves in some ways like a reflexive pronoun. For example, a direct object *each other* must refer to the subject, and a subject *each other* cannot refer to the direct object:

(i) They like each other.

(ii)*Each other like(s) them.

    A. Construct examples parallel to those in (1)–(3), replacing the reflexives with reciprocals. Is the basic behavior of reciprocals similar to that of reflexives?

    B. Construct examples parallel to those in (5)–(7), replacing the reflexives with reciprocals. Is the behavior of reciprocals similar to that of reflexives in imperative sentences and in sentences containing *appeal* and *appear*?

    C. Are there any constraints that the reciprocal imposes on its antecedent that reflexives don't impose? [*Hint: what change to (1d) and (6b) did you have to make in order to construct the corresponding well formed reciprocal sentence?*]

    D. Consider the following contrast:

        They lost each other's books.

        *They lost themselves' books.

    Discuss how such examples bear on the applicability of Hypothesis III to reciprocals. [*Hint: before you answer the question, think about what the verbal arguments are in the above sentences.*]

You can see that things get quite complex quite fast, requiring abstract notions like 'coreference', being 'arguments of the same verb', and allowing arguments to be missing from the sentence but 'understood', for purposes of the rules for pronoun type. And we've only scratched the surface of this problem. For example, all the versions of the rules we have come up with so far predict that nonreflexive forms of a pronoun should appear only in positions where their reflexive counterparts are impossible. But this is not quite true, as the following examples illustrate:

(8) a. We wrapped the blankets around us.
    b. We wrapped the blankets around ourselves.
    c. We admired the pictures of us in the album.
    d. We admired the pictures of ourselves in the album.

It should be evident by now that formulating precise rules characterizing where English speakers use reflexive pronouns and where they use nonreflexive pronouns will be a difficult task. We will return to this task in Chapter 7. Our reason for discussing it here was to emphasize the following points:

- Normal use of language involves the mastery of a complex system, which is not directly accessible to consciousness.
- Speakers' tacit knowledge of language can be studied by formulating hypotheses and testing their predictions against intuitive judgments of well formedness.
- The theoretical machinery required for a viable grammatical analysis could be quite abstract.

1.3   Remarks on the History of the Study of Grammar

The conception of grammar we've just presented is quite a recent development. Until about 1800, almost all linguistics was primarily prescriptive. Traditional grammar (going back hundreds, even thousands of years, to ancient India and ancient Greece) was developed largely in response to the inevitable changing of language, which is always (even today) seen by most people as its deterioration. Prescriptive grammars have always been attempts to codify the 'correct' way of talking. Hence, they have concentrated on relatively peripheral aspects of language structure. On the other hand, they have also provided many useful concepts for the sort of grammar we'll be doing. For example, our notion of parts of speech, as well as the most familiar examples (such as *noun* and *verb*) come from the ancient Greeks.

A critical turning point in the history of linguistics took place at the end of the eighteenth century. It was discovered at that time that there was a historical connection among most of the languages of Europe, as well as Sanskrit and other languages of India (plus some languages in between).[5] This led to a tremendous flowering of the field of historical linguistics, centered on reconstructing the family tree of the Indo-European languages by comparing the modern languages with each other and with older texts. Most of this effort concerned the correspondences between individual words and the sounds within those words. But syntactic comparison and reconstruction was also initiated during this period.

In the early twentieth century, many linguists, following the lead of the Swiss scholar Ferdinand de Saussure, turned their attention from the historical (or 'diachronic'[6]) study to the 'synchronic'[7] analysis of languages – that is, to the characterization of languages at a given point in time. The attention to synchronic studies encouraged the investigation of languages that had no writing systems, which are much harder to study diachronically since there is no record of their earlier forms.

In the United States, these developments led linguists to pay far more attention to the indigenous languages of the Americas. Beginning with the work of the anthropological linguist Franz Boas, American linguistics for the first half of the twentieth century was very much concerned with the immense diversity of languages. The Indo-European languages, which were the focus of most nineteenth-century linguistic research, constitute only a tiny fraction of the approximately five thousand known languages. In broadening this perspective, American linguists put great stress on developing ways to describe languages that would not forcibly impose the structure of a familiar language (such as Latin or English) on something very different; most, though by no means all, of this work emphasized the differences among languages. Some linguists, notably Edward Sapir and Benjamin Lee Whorf, talked about how language could provide insights into how people think. They tended to emphasize alleged differences among the thought patterns of speakers of different languages. For our purposes, their most important claim is that the structure of language can provide insight into human cognitive processes. This idea has wide currency today, and, as we shall see below, it constitutes one of the most interesting motivations for studying syntax.

In the period around World War II, a number of things happened to set the stage for a revolutionary change in the study of syntax. One was that great advances in mathematical logic provided formal tools that seemed well suited for application to studying natural languages.

---

[5]The discovery is often attributed to Sir William Jones who announced such a relationship in a 1786 address, but others had noted affinities among these languages before him.

[6]From the Greek: *dia* 'across' plus *chronos* 'time'

[7]*syn* 'same, together' plus *chronos*.

A related development was the invention of the computer. Though early computers were unbelievably slow and expensive by today's standards, some people immediately saw their potential for natural language applications, such as machine translation or voice typewriters.

A third relevant development around mid-century was the decline of behaviorism in the social sciences. Like many other disciplines, linguistics in America at that time was dominated by behaviorist thinking. That is, it was considered unscientific to posit mental entities or states to account for human behaviors; everything was supposed to be described in terms of correlations between stimuli and responses. Abstract models of what might be going on inside people's minds were taboo. Around 1950, some psychologists began to question these methodological restrictions, and arguing they made it impossible to explain certain kinds of facts. This set the stage for a serious rethinking of the goals and methods of linguistic research.

In the early 1950s, a young man named Noam Chomsky entered the field of linguistics. In the late '50s, he published three things that revolutionized the study of syntax. One was a set of mathematical results, establishing the foundations of what is now called 'formal language theory'. These results have been seminal in theoretical computer science, and they are crucial underpinnings for computational work on natural language. The second was a book called *Syntactic Structures* that presented a new formalism for grammatical description and analyzed a substantial fragment of English in terms of that formalism. The third was a review of B. F. Skinner's (1957) book *Verbal Behavior*. Skinner was one of the most influential psychologists of the time, an extreme behaviorist. Chomsky's scathing and devastating review marks, in many people's minds, the end of behaviorism's dominance in American social science.

Since about 1960, Chomsky has been the dominant figure in linguistics. As it happens, the 1960s were a period of unprecedented growth in American academia. Most linguistics departments in the United States were established in the period between 1960 and 1980. This helped solidify Chomsky's dominant position.

One of the central tenets of the Chomskyan approach to syntax, known as 'generative grammar', has already been introduced: hypotheses about linguistic structure should be made precise enough to be testable. A second somewhat more controversial one is that the object of study should be the unconscious knowledge underlying ordinary language use. A third fundamental claim of Chomsky's concerns the biological basis of human linguistic abilities. We will return to this claim in the next section.

Within these general guidelines there is room for many different theories of grammar. Since the 1950s, generative grammarians have explored a wide variety of choices of formalism and theoretical vocabulary. We present a brief summary of these in Appendix B, to help situate the approach presented here within a broader intellectual landscape.

1.4 Why Study Syntax?

Students in syntax courses often ask about the point of such classes: why should one study syntax?

Of course, one has to distinguish this question from a closely related one: why DO people study syntax? The answer to that question is perhaps simpler: exploring the structure of language is an intellectually challenging and, for many people, intrinsically fascinating activity. It is like working on a gigantic puzzle – one so large that it could occupy many lifetimes. Thus, as in any scientific discipline, many researchers are simply captivated by the complex mysteries presented by the data themselves – in this case a seemingly endless, diverse array of languages past, present and future.

This reason is, of course, similar to the reason scholars in any scientific field pursue their research: natural curiosity and fascination with some domain of study. Basic research is not typically driven by the possibility of applications. Although looking for results that will be useful in the short term might be the best strategy for someone seeking personal fortune, it wouldn't be the best strategy for a society looking for long-term benefit from the scientific research it supports. Basic scientific investigation has proven over the centuries to have long-term payoffs, even when the applications were not evident at the time the research was carried out. For example, work in logic and the foundations of mathematics in the first decades of the twentieth century laid the theoretical foundations for the development of the digital computer, but the scholars who did this work were not concerned with its possible applications. Likewise, we don't believe there is any need for linguistic research to be justified on the basis of its foreseeable uses. Nonetheless, we will mention three interrelated reasons that one might have for studying the syntax of human languages.

1.4.1 A Window on the Structure of the Mind

One intellectually important rationale for the study of syntax has been offered by Chomsky. In essence, it is that language – and particularly, its grammatical organization – can provide an especially clear window on the structure of the human mind.[8]

Chomsky claims that the most remarkable fact about human language is the discrepancy between its apparent complexity and the ease with which children acquire it. The structure of any natural language is far more complicated than those of artificial languages or of even the most sophisticated mathematical systems. Yet learning computer languages or mathematics requires intensive instruction (and many students still never master them), whereas every normal child learns at least one natural language merely through exposure. This amazing fact cries out for explanation.[9]

Chomsky's proposed explanation is that most of the complexity of languages does not have to be learned, because much of our knowledge of it is innate: we are born knowing about it. That is, our brains are 'hardwired' to learn languages of certain types.

More generally, Chomsky has argued that the human mind is highly modular. That is, we have special-purpose 'mental organs' that are designed to do particular sorts of tasks in particular sorts of ways. The language organ (which, in Chomsky's view, has several largely autonomous submodules) is of particular interest because language is such a pervasive and unique part of human nature. All people use language, and (he claims) no other species is capable of learning anything much like human language. Hence, in studying the structure of human languages, we are investigating a central aspect of human nature.

This idea has drawn enormous attention not only from linguists but also from people outside linguistics, especially psychologists and philosophers. Scholars in these fields have been highly divided about Chomsky's innateness claims. Many cognitive psychologists see Chomsky's work as a model for how other mental faculties should be studied, while others argue that the mind (or brain) should be regarded as a general-purpose thinking device, without specialized modules. In philosophy, Chomsky provoked much comment by claiming that his work constitutes a modern version of Descartes' doctrine of innate ideas.

Chomsky's innateness thesis and the interdisciplinary dialogue it stimulated were major factors in the birth of the new interdisciplinary field of cognitive science in the 1970s. (An even more important factor was the rapid evolution of computers, with the concomitant growth

---

[8]See Katz and Postal (1991) for arguments against the dominant Chomskyan conception of linguistics as essentially concerned with psychological facts.

[9]Chomsky was certainly not the first person to remark on the extraordinary facility with which children learn language, but, by giving it a central place in his work, he has focused considerable attention on it.

of artificial intelligence and the idea that the computer could be used as a model of the mind.) Chomsky and his followers have been major contributors to cognitive science in the subsequent decades.

One theoretical consequence of Chomsky's innateness claim is that all languages must share most of their structure. This is because all children learn the languages spoken around them, irrespective of where their ancestors came from. Hence, the innate knowledge that Chomsky claims makes language acquisition possible must be common to all human beings. If this knowledge also determines most aspects of grammatical structure, as Chomsky says it does, then all languages must be essentially alike. This is a very strong universal claim.

In fact, Chomsky tends to use the term 'Universal Grammar' to mean the innate endowment that permits language acquisition. A great deal of the syntactic research since the late 1960s has been concerned with identifying linguistic universals, especially those that could plausibly be claimed to reflect innate mental structures operative in language acquisition. As we proceed to develop the grammar in this text, we will ask which aspects of our grammar are peculiar to English and which might plausibly be considered universal.

If Chomsky is right about the innateness of the language faculty, it has a number of practical consequences, especially in fields like language instruction and therapy for language disorders. For example, since there is evidence that people's innate ability to learn languages is far more powerful very early in life (specifically, before puberty) than later, it seems most sensible that elementary education should have a heavy emphasis on language, and that foreign language instruction should not be left until secondary school, as it is in most American schools today.

1.4.2 A Window on the Mind's Activity

If you stop and think about it, it's really quite amazing that people succeed in communicating by using language. Language seems to have a number of design properties that get in the way of efficient and accurate communication of the kind that routinely takes place.

First, it is massively ambiguous. Individual words, for example, often have not just one but a number of meanings, as illustrated by the English examples in (9).

(9) a. Leslie used a *pen*. ('a writing implement')
     b. We put the pigs in a *pen*. ('a fenced enclosure')
     c. They should *pen* the letter quickly. ('to write')
     d. The judge sent them to the *pen* for a decade. ('a penitentiary')

(10) a. The cheetah will *run* down the hill. ('to move fast')
     b. The president will *run*. ('to be a political candidate')
     c. The car won't *run*. ('to function properly')
     d. This trail should *run* over the hill. ('to lead')
     e. This dye will *run*. ('to dissolve and spread')
     f. This room will *run* $200 or more. ('to cost')
     g. She can *run* an accelerator. ('to operate')
     h. They will *run* the risk. ('to incur')
     i. These stockings will *run*. ('to tear')
     j. There is a *run* in that stocking. ('a tear')
     k. We need another *run* to win. ('a score in baseball')
     l. Fats won with a *run* of 20. ('a sequence of successful shots in a game of pool')

To make matters worse, many sentences are ambiguous not because they contain ambiguous words, but rather because the words they contain can be related to one another in more than one way, as illustrated in (11).

(11) a. Lee saw the student with a telescope.
     b. I forgot how good beer tastes.

(11a) can be interpreted as providing information about which student Lee saw (the one with a telescope) or about what instrument Lee used (the telescope) to see the student. Similarly, (11b) can convey either that the speaker forgot how GOOD beer (as opposed to bad or mediocre beer) tastes, or else that the speaker forgot that beer (in general) tastes good. These differences are often discussed in terms of which element a word like *with* or *good* is modifying (the verb or the noun).

Lexical and modificational ambiguity interact to produce a bewildering array of (often comical) ambiguities, like these:

(12) a. Visiting relatives can be boring.
     b. If only Superman would stop flying planes!
     c. That's a new car dealership.
     d. I know you like the back of my hand.
     e. An earthquake in Romania moved buildings as far away as Moscow and Rome.
     f. The German shepherd turned on its master.
     g. I saw that gas can explode.
     h. Max is on the phone now.
     i. The only thing capable of consuming this food has four legs and flies.
     j. I saw her duck.

Problem 4: Ambiguity
Give a brief description of each ambiguity illustrated in (12). We will return to many of these examples – or closely related ones – later in the book.

This is not the end of the worrisome design properties of human language. Many words are used to refer to different things on different occasions of utterance. Pronouns like *them*, *(s)he*, *this*, and *that* pick out different referents almost every time they are used. Even seemingly determinate pronouns like *we* don't pin down exactly which set of people the speaker is referring to (compare *We have two kids/a city council/a lieutenant governor/50 states/oxygen-based life here*). Moreover, although certain proper names like *Sally Ride* or *Sandra Day O'Connor* might reliably pick out the same person almost every time they are used, most conversations are full of uses of names like *Chris, Pat, Leslie, Sandy, Bo*, etc. that vary wildly in their reference, depending on who's talking to whom and what they're talking about.

Add to this the observation that some expressions seem to make reference to 'covert elements' that don't exactly correspond to any one word. So expressions like *in charge* and *afterwards* make reference to missing elements of some kind – bits of the meaning that have to be supplied from context. Otherwise, discourses like the following wouldn't make sense, or would at best be incomplete.

(13) a. I'm creating a committee. Kim – you're in charge. [in charge of what? – the committee]

b. Lights go out at ten. There will be no talking afterwards. [after what? – after ten]

The way something is said can also have a significant effect on the meaning expressed. A rising intonation, for example, on a one word utterance like *Coffee?* would very naturally convey 'Do you want some coffee?' Alternatively, it might be used to convey that 'coffee' is being offered as a tentative answer to some question (say, *What was Columbia's former number-one cash crop?*). Or even, in the right context, the same utterance might be used in seeking confirmation that a given liquid was in fact coffee. Intonational meaning can be vivified in striking ways.

Finally, note that communication using language leaves a great deal unsaid. If I say to you *Can you give me a hand here?* I'm not just requesting information about your abilities, I'm asking you to help me out. This is the unmistakable communicative intent, but it wasn't literally said. Other examples of such inference are similar, but perhaps more subtle. A famous example[10] is the letter of recommendation saying that the candidate in question has outstanding penmanship (and saying nothing more than that!).

Summing all this up, what we have just seen is that the messages conveyed by utterances of sentences are multiply ambiguous, vague, and uncertain. Yet somehow, in spite of this, those of us who know the language are able to use it to transmit messages to one another with considerable accuracy – far more accuracy than the language itself would seem to permit. Those readers who have any experience with computer programming or with mathematical logic will appreciate this dilemma instantly. The very idea of designing a programming language or a logical language whose predicates are ambiguous or whose variables are left without assigned values is unthinkable. No computer can process linguistic expressions unless it 'knows' precisely what the expressions mean and what to do with them.

The fact of the matter is that human language-users are able to do something that modern science doesn't understand well enough to replicate via computer. Somehow, people are able to use nonlinguistic information in such a way that they are never even aware of most of the unwanted interpretations of words, phrases, and sentences. Consider again the various senses of the word *pen*. The 'writing implement' sense is more common – that is, more frequent in the language you've been exposed to (unless you're a farmer or a prisoner) – and so there is an inherent bias toward that sense. You can think of this in terms of 'weighting' or 'degrees of activation' of word senses. In a context where farm animals are being discussed, though, the weights shift – the senses more closely associated with the subject matter of the discourse become stronger in this case. As people direct their attention to and through a given dialogue, these sense preferences can fluctuate considerably. The human sense selection capability is incredibly robust, yet we have only minimal understanding of the cognitive mechanisms that are at work. How exactly does context facilitate our ability to locate the correct sense?

In other cases, it's hard to explain disambiguation so easily in terms of affinity to the domain of discourse. Consider the following contrast:

(14) a. They found the book on the table.
      b. They found the book on the atom.

---

[10]This example is one of many due to the late H. Paul Grice, the philosopher whose work forms the starting point for much work in linguistics on problems of PRAGMATICS, how people 'read between the lines' in natural conversation; see Grice (1989).

The preposition *on* modifies the verb in (14a) and the noun in (14b), yet it seems that nothing short of rather complex reasoning about the relative size of objects would enable someone to choose which meaning (i.e. which modification) made sense. And we do this kind of thing very quickly, as you can see from (15).

(15) After finding the book on the atom, Sandy went into class, confident that there would be no further obstacles to getting that term paper done.

When you read this sentence, there's no strong feeling that you were 'garden pathed', that is, derailed by an incorrect interpretation midsentence. The decision about how to construe *on the atom* is made well before the words *class* or *confident* are even encountered.

When we process language, we integrate encyclopedic knowledge, plausibility information, frequency biases, discourse information, and perhaps more. Although we don't yet know exactly how we do it, it's clear that we do it very quickly and reasonably accurately. Trying to model this integration is probably the most important research task facing the study of language in the coming millennium.

Syntax plays a crucial role in all this. It imposes constraints on how sentences can or cannot be construed. So the discourse context may provide a bias for the 'fenced enclosure' sense of *pen*, but it is the syntactic context that determines whether *pen* occurs as a noun or a verb. Syntax is also of particular importance to the development of language-processing models, because it is a domain of knowledge that can be characterized perhaps more precisely than some of the other kinds of knowledge that are involved.

When we understand how language processing works, we probably will also understand quite a bit more about how cognitive processes work in general. This in turn will no doubt enable us to develop better ways of teaching language. We should also be better able to help people who have communicative impairments (and more general cognitive disorders). The study of human language-processing is an important sub-area of the study of human cognition, and it is one that can benefit immensely from precise characterization of linguistic knowledge of the sort that syntacticians seek to provide.

1.4.3 Natural Language Technologies

Grammar has more utilitarian applications, as well. One of the most promising areas for applying syntactic research is in the development of useful and robust natural language technologies. What do we mean by 'natural language technologies'? Roughly, what we have in mind is any sort of computer application that involves natural languages like English, Japanese, or Swahili in essential ways. These include devices that translate from one language into another (or perhaps more realistically, that provide translation assistance to someone with less than perfect command of a language), that understand spoken language (to varying degrees), that automatically retrieve information from large bodies of text stored on-line, or that help the disabled to communicate.

There is one application that obviously must incorporate a great deal of grammatical information, namely, grammar checkers for word processing. Most modern word processing systems include a grammar checking facility, along with a spell-checker. These tend to focus on the concerns of prescriptive grammar, which may be appropriate for the sorts of documents they are generally used on, but which often leads to spurious 'corrections'. Moreover, they typically depend on superficial pattern-matching for finding likely grammatical errors, rather than employing in-depth grammatical analysis. In short, grammar checkers can benefit from incorporating the results of research in syntax.

Other computer applications in which grammatical knowledge is clearly essential include those in which well formed natural language output must be generated. For example, reliable software for translating one language into another must incorporate some representation of the grammar of the target language. If it did not, it would either produce ill-formed output, or it would be limited to some fixed repertoire of sentence templates.

Even where usable natural language technologies can be developed that are not informed by grammatical research, it is often the case that they can be made more robust by including a principled syntactic component. For example, Stanford University's Center for the Study of Language and Information is developing software to reduce the number of keystrokes needed to input text. This has many potential uses, including facilitating the use of computers by individuals with motor disabilities or temporary impairments such as carpal tunnel syndrome. It is clear that knowledge of the grammar of English can help in predicting what words are likely to come next at an arbitrary point in a sentence. Software that makes such predictions and offers the user a set of choices for the next word or the remainder of an entire sentence – each of which can be inserted with a single keystroke – can be of great value in a wide variety of situations. Word prediction can likewise facilitate the disambiguation of noisy signals in continuous speech recognition and handwriting recognition.

But it's not obvious that all types of natural language technologies need to be sensitive to grammatical information. Say, for example, we were trying to design a system to extract information from an online database by typing in English questions (rather than requiring use of a special database query language, as is the case with most existing database systems). Some computer scientists have argued that full grammatical analysis of the queries is not necessary. Instead, they claim, all that is needed is a program that can extract the essential semantic information out of the queries. Many grammatical details don't seem necessary in order to understand the queries, so it has been argued that they can be ignored for the purpose of this application. Even here, however, a strong case can be made for the value of including a syntactic component in the software.

To see why, imagine that we are using a database in a law office, containing information about the firm's past and present cases, including records of witnesses' testimony. Without designing the query system to pay careful attention to certain details of English grammar, there are questions we might want to ask of this database that could be misanalyzed and hence answered incorrectly. For example, consider our old friend, the rule for reflexive and nonreflexive pronouns. Since formal database query languages don't make any such distinction, one might think it wouldn't be necessary for an English interface to do so either. But suppose we asked one of the following questions:

(16) a.   Which witnesses work with defendants who supervise them?
      b.   Which witnesses work with defendants who supervise themselves?

Obviously, these two questions will have different answers, so an English language 'front end' that didn't incorporate some rules for distinguishing reflexive and nonreflexive pronouns would sometimes give wrong answers.

In fact, it isn't enough to tell reflexive from nonreflexive pronouns: a database system would need to be able to tell different reflexive pronouns apart. The next two sentences, for example, are identical except for the plurality of the reflexive pronouns:

(17) a.   List all witnesses for the defendant who represented himself.
      b.   List all witnesses for the defendant who represented themselves.

Again, the appropriate answers would be different. So a system that didn't pay attention to whether pronouns are singular or plural couldn't be trusted to answer correctly.

Even features of English grammar that seem useless – things that appear to be entirely redundant – are needed for the analysis of some sentences that might well be used in a human-computer interaction.

Consider, for example, English subject-verb agreement (a topic we will return to in some detail in Chapters 2–4). Since subjects are marked as singular or plural – *the dog* vs. *the dogs* – marking verbs for the same thing – *barks* vs. *bark* – seems to add nothing. We would have little trouble understanding someone who always left subject agreement off of verbs. In fact, English doesn't even mark past-tense verbs (other than forms of *be*) for subject agreement. But we don't miss agreement in the past tense, because it is semantically redundant. One might conjecture, therefore, that an English database querying system might be able simply to ignore agreement.

However, once again, examples can be constructed in which the agreement marking on the verb is the only indicator of a crucial semantic distinction. This is the case with the following pair:

(18) a.   List associates of each witness who speaks Spanish.
      b.   List associates of each witness who speak Spanish.

In the first sentence, it is the witnesses in question who are the Spanish-speakers; in the second, it is their associates. These will, in general, not lead to the same answer.

Such examples could be multiplied, but these should be enough to make the point: Building truly robust natural language technologies – that is, software that will allow you to interact with your computer in YOUR language, rather than in ITS language – requires careful and detailed analysis of grammatical structure and how it influences meaning. Shortcuts that rely on semantic heuristics, guesses, or simple pattern-matching will inevitably make mistakes.

Of course, this is not to deny the value of clever engineering and statistical approximation. Indeed, the rapid emergence of natural language technology that is taking place in the world today owes at least as much to this as it does to the insights of linguistic research. Our point is rather that in the long run, especially when the tasks to be performed take on more linguistic subtlety and the accuracy of the performance becomes more critical, the need for more subtle linguistic analysis will likewise become more acute.

In short, although most linguists may be motivated primarily by simple intellectual curiosity, the study of grammar has some fairly obvious uses, even in the relatively short term.

1.5   Conclusion

In this chapter, we have drawn an important distinction between prescriptive and descriptive grammar. In addition, we provided an illustration of the kind of syntactic puzzles we will focus on later in the text.[11] Finally, we provided an overview of some of the reasons people have found the study of syntax inherently interesting or useful. In the next chapter, we look at some simple formal models that might be proposed for the grammars of natural languages and discuss some of their shortcomings.

1.6 Further Reading

An entertaining and knowledgeable exposition of modern linguistics and its implications is provided by Pinker (1994). A somewhat more scholarly survey with a slightly different focus is presented by Jackendoff (1994). For discussion of prescriptive grammar, see Nunberg (1983) and Chapter 12 of Pinker's book (an edited version of which was published in *The New Republic*, January 31, 1994). For an overview of linguistic science in the nineteenth century, see Pedersen (1959). A succinct survey of the history of linguistics is provided by Robins (1967).

Among Chomsky's many writings on the implications of language acquisition for the study of the mind, we would especially recommend Chomsky (1959) and Chomsky (1972); a more recent, but much more difficult work is Chomsky (1986a). There have been few recent attempts at surveying work in (human or machine) sentence processing. J. A. Fodor, Bever, and Garrett (1974) is a comprehensive review of early psycholinguistic work within the Chomskyan paradigm, but it is now quite dated. Garrett (1990) and J. D. Fodor (1995) are more recent, but much more limited in scope.

---

[11] Our discussion of reflexive and nonreflexive pronouns borrows heavily from the presentation in Perlmutter and Soames (1979: chapters 2 and 3).

2

Some Simple Theories of Grammar

2.1 Introduction

Among the key points in the previous chapter were the following:

- Language is rule-governed.
- The rules aren't the ones we were taught in school.
- Much of our linguistic knowledge is unconscious, so we have to get at it indirectly; one way of doing this is to consult intuitions of what sounds good.

In this text, we have a number of objectives. First, we will work toward developing a set of rules that will correctly predict the acceptability of (a large subset of) English sentences. The ultimate goal is a grammar that can tell us for any arbitrary string of English words whether or not it is a well-formed sentence. Thus we will again and again be engaged in the exercise of formulating a grammar that generates a certain set of word strings – the sentences predicted to be grammatical according to that grammar. We will then examine particular members of that set and ask ourselves: 'Is this example acceptable?' The goal of this enterprise is to make the set of sentences generated by our grammar match the set of sentences that we intuitively judge to be acceptable.[1]

A second of our objectives is to consider how the grammar of English differs from the grammar of other languages (or how the grammar of standard American English differs from those of other varieties of English). The conception of grammar we develop will involve general principles that are just as applicable (as we will see in various exercises)

---

[1] Of course there may be other interacting factors that cause grammatical sentences to sound less than fully acceptable – see Chapter 9 for further discussion. In addition, we don't all speak exactly the same variety of English, though we will assume that existing varieties are sufficiently similar for us to engage in a meaningful discussion of quite a bit of English grammar.

to superficially different languages as they are to English. Ultimately, as we will see, much of the outward differences among languages can be viewed as lexical in nature.

Finally, as we develop grammars that include principles of considerable generality, we will begin to see constructs that may have universal applicability to human language. So one of our goals will be to consider what our findings might tell us about human linguistic abilities in general.

In developing the informal rules for reflexive and nonreflexive pronouns in Chapter 1, we assumed that we already knew a lot about the structure of the sentences we were looking at – that is, we talked about subjects, objects, clauses, etc. In fact, a fully worked out theory of reflexive and nonreflexive pronouns is going to require that many other aspects of syntactic theory get worked out first. We begin this grammar development process in the present chapter.

We will consider several candidates for theories of English grammar. We begin by quickly dismissing certain simple-minded approaches. We spend more time on a formalism known as 'context-free grammar', which serves as a starting point for most modern theories of syntax. A brief overview of some of the most important schools of thought within the paradigm of generative grammar, situating the approach developed in this text with respect to some alternatives, is included in Appendix B.

2.2 Two Simplistic Syntactic Theories

2.2.1 Lists as Grammars

The simplest imaginable syntactic theory is that a grammar consists of a list of all the well-formed sentences in the language. The most obvious problem with such a proposal is that the list would have to be too long. There is no fixed finite bound on the length of English sentences, as can be seen from the following sequence:

(1) Some sentences go on and on.
   Some sentences go on and on and on.
   Some sentences go on and on and on and on.
   Some sentences go on and on and on and on and on.

   . . .

Every sentence in this sequence is acceptable English. Since there is no bound on their size, it follows that the number of sentences in the list must be infinite. Hence there are infinitely many sentences of English. Since human brains are finite, they cannot store infinite lists. Consequently, there must be some more compact way of encoding the grammatical knowledge that speakers of English possess.

Moreover, there are generalizations about the structure of English that an adequate grammar should express. For example, consider a hypothetical language consisting of infinitely many sentences similar to those in (1), except that every other sentence reversed the order of the words *some* and *sentences*:[2]

(2)   Some sentences go on and on.
        *Sentences some go on and on.
        *Some sentences go on and on and on.
        Sentences some go on and on and on.
        Some sentences go on and on and on and on.
        *Sentences some go on and on and on and on.
        *Some sentences go on and on and on and on and on.
        Sentences some go on and on and on and on and on. ...

Of course, none of these sentences[3] where the word *sentences* precedes the word *some* is a well-formed English sentence. Moreover, no natural language exhibits patterns of that sort – in this case, having word order depend on whether the length of the sentence is divisible by 4. A syntactic theory that sheds light on human linguistic abilities ought to explain why such patterns do not occur in human languages. But a theory that said grammars consisted of lists of sentences could not do that. If grammars were just lists, then there would be no patterns that would be excluded – and none that would be expected, either.

This form of argument – that a certain theory of grammar fails to 'capture a linguistically significant generalization' is very common in generative grammar. It takes for granted the idea that language is 'rule governed', that is, that language is a combinatoric system whose operations are 'out there' to be discovered by empirical investigation. If a particular characterization of the way a language works leads to excessive redundancy and complications, it's assumed to be the wrong characterization of the grammar of that language. We will see this kind of argumentation again, in connection with more plausible proposals than the idea that grammars simply list sentences. In Chapter 9, we will argue that (perhaps surprisingly), a grammar motivated largely on the basis of such parsimony considerations seems to be a good candidate for a psychological model of the knowledge of language that is employed in speaking and understanding.

---

[2]The asterisks in (2) are intended to indicate the ungrammaticality of the strings in the hypothetical language under discussion, not in normal English.

[3]Note that we are already slipping into a common, but imprecise, way of talking about unacceptable strings of words as 'sentences'.

2.2.2 Regular Expressions

A natural first step toward allowing grammars to capture generalizations is to classify words into what are often called 'parts of speech' or 'grammatical categories'. There are large numbers of words that behave similarly syntactically. For example, the words *apple, book, color,* and *dog* all can appear in roughly the same contexts, such as the following:

(3) a. That __ surprised me.
    b. I noticed the __.
    c. They were interested in his __.
    d. This is my favorite __.

Moreover, they all have plural forms that can be constructed in similar ways (orthographically, simply by adding an -*s*).

Traditionally, the vocabulary of a language is sorted into nouns, verbs, etc. based on loose semantic characterizations (e.g. 'a noun is a word that refers to a person, place, or thing'). While there is undoubtedly a grain of insight at the heart of such definitions, we can make use of this division into grammatical categories without committing ourselves to any semantic basis for them. For our purposes, it is sufficient that there are classes of words that may occur grammatically in the same environments. Our theory of grammar can capture their common behavior by formulating patterns or rules in terms of categories, not individual words.

Someone might, then, propose that the grammar of English is a list of patterns, stated in terms of grammatical categories, together with a lexicon – that is, a list of words and their categories. For example, the patterns could include (among many others):

(4) a. ARTICLE NOUN VERB
    b. ARTICLE NOUN VERB ARTICLE NOUN

And the lexicon could include (likewise, among many others):

(5) a. Articles: a, the
    b. Nouns: cat, dog
    c. Verbs: attacked, scratched

This mini-grammar licenses forty well-formed English sentences, and captures a few generalizations. However, a grammar that consists of a list of patterns still suffers from the first drawback of the theory of grammars as lists of sentences: it can only account for a finite number of sentences, while a natural language is an infinite set of sentences. For example, such a grammar will still be incapable of dealing with all of the sentences in the infinite sequence illustrated in (1).

We can enhance our theory of grammar so as to permit infinite numbers of sentences by introducing a device that extends its descriptive power. In particular, the problem associated with (2) can be handled using what is known as the 'Kleene star'.[4] Notated as a superscripted asterisk, the Kleene star is interpreted to mean that the expression it is attached to can be repeated any finite number of times (including zero). Thus, the examples in (1) could be abbreviated as follows:

(6) Some sentences go on and on [and on]*.

A closely related notation is a superscripted plus sign (called Kleene plus), meaning that one or more occurrences of the expression it is attached to are permissible. Hence, another way of expressing the same pattern would be:

(7) Some sentences go on [and on]+.

We shall employ these, as well as two common abbreviatory devices. The first is simply to put parentheses around material that is optional. For example, the two sentence patterns in (4) could be collapsed into: ARTICLE NOUN VERB (ARTICLE NOUN). The second abbreviatory device is a vertical bar, which is used to separate alternatives.[5] For example, if we wished to expand the mini-grammar in (4) to include sentences like *The dog looked angry*, we could add the pattern ARTICLE NOUN VERB ADJECTIVE and collapse it with the previous patterns as: ARTICLE NOUN VERB (ARTICLE NOUN)|ADJECTIVE. Of course, we would also have to add the verb *looked* and the adjective *angry* to the lexicon.[6]

Patterns making use of the devices just described – Kleene star, Kleene plus, parentheses for optionality, and the vertical bar for alternatives – are known as 'regular expressions'.[7] A great deal is known about what sorts of patterns can and cannot be represented with regular expressions (see, for example, Hopcroft and Ullman (1979; chaps. 2 and 3)), and a number of scholars have argued that natural lan-

---

[4]Named after the logician Stephen Kleene.

[5]This is the notation standardly used in computer science and in the study of mathematical properties of grammatical systems. Descriptive linguists tend to use curly brackets to annotate alternatives.

[6]This extension of the grammar would license some unacceptable strings, e.g. *The cat scratched angry*. This sort of overgeneration is always a danger when extending a grammar, as we will see in subsequent chapters.

[7]This is not intended as a rigorous definition of regular expressions. A precise definition would include the requirement that the empty string is a regular expression, and would probably omit some of the devices mentioned in the text (because they can be defined in terms of others). Incidentally, readers who use computers with the UNIX operating system may be familiar with the command 'grep'. This stands for 'Global Regular Expression Printer'.

guages in fact exhibit patterns that are beyond the descriptive capacity of regular expressions (see Bar-Hillel and Shamir (1960; secs. 5 and 6)). The most convincing arguments for employing a grammatical formalism richer than regular expressions, however, have to do with the need to capture generalizations.

In (4), the string ARTICLE NOUN occurs twice, once before the verb and once after it. Notice that there are other options possible in both of these positions:

(8) a. *Dogs* chase *cats.*
    b. *A large dog* chased *a small cat.*
    c. *A dog with brown spots* chased *a cat with no tail.*

Moreover, these are not the only positions in which the same strings can occur:

(9) a. Some people yell at *(the) (noisy) dogs (in my neighborhood).*
    b. Some people consider *(the) (noisy) dogs (in my neighborhood)* dangerous.

Even with the abbreviatory devices available in regular expressions, the same lengthy string of symbols – something like (ARTICLE) (ADJEC-TIVE) NOUN (PREPOSITION ARTICLE NOUN) – will have to appear over and over again in the patterns that constitute the grammar. Moreover, the recurring patterns are in fact considerably more complicated than those illustrated so far. Strings of other forms, such as *the noisy annoying dogs, the dogs that live in my neighborhood,* or *Rover, Fido, and Lassie* can all occur in just the same positions. It would clearly simplify the grammar if we could give this apparently infinite set of strings a name and say that any string from the set can appear in certain positions in a sentence.

Furthermore, as we have already seen, an adequate theory of syntax must somehow account for the fact that a given string of words can sometimes be put together in more than one way. If there is no more to grammar than lists of recurring patterns, where these are defined in terms of parts of speech, then there is no apparent way to talk about the ambiguity of sentences like those in (10).

(10) a. We enjoyed the movie with Cher.
     b. The room was filled with noisy children and animals.
     c. People with children who use drugs should be locked up.
     d. I saw the astronomer with a telescope.

In the first sentence, it can be us or the movie that is 'with Cher'; in the second, it can be either just the children or both the children and the animals that are noisy; in the third, it can be the children or their parents who use drugs, and so forth. None of these ambiguities can be plausibly attributed to a lexical ambiguity. Rather, they seem to result from different ways of grouping the words into phrases.

In short, the fundamental defect of regular expressions as a theory of grammar is that they provide no means for representing the fact that a string of several words may constitute a unit. The same holds true of several other formalisms that are provably equivalent to regular expressions (including what is known as 'finite-state grammar').

The recurrent strings we have been seeing are usually called 'phrases' or '(syntactic) constituents'.[8] Phrases, like words, come in different types. All of the italicized phrases in (8)–(9) above obligatorily include a noun, so they are called 'Noun Phrases'. The next natural enrichment of our theory of grammar is to permit our regular expressions to include not only words and parts of speech, but also phrase types. Then we also need to provide (similarly enriched) regular expressions to provide the patterns for each type of phrase. The technical name for this theory of grammar is 'Context-free Phrase Structure Grammar' or simply 'Context-free Grammar', sometimes abbreviated as CFG. CFGs, which will also let us begin to talk about structural ambiguity like that illustrated in (10), form the starting point for most serious attempts to develop formal grammars for natural languages.

2.3 Context-free Phrase Structure Grammar

The term 'grammatical category' now covers not only the parts of speech, but also types of phrases, such as noun phrase and prepositional phrase. To distinguish the two types, we will sometimes use the terms 'lexical category' (for parts of speech) and 'nonlexical category' or 'phrasal category' to mean types of phrases. For convenience, we will abbreviate them, so that 'NOUN' becomes 'N', 'NOUN PHRASE' becomes 'NP', etc.

A context-free phrase structure grammar has two parts:

- A LEXICON, consisting of a list of words, with their associated grammatical categories.[9]
- A set of RULES of the form $A \rightarrow \varphi$ where A is a nonlexical category,

---

[8]There is a minor difference in the way these terms are used: linguists often use 'phrase' in contrast to 'word' to mean something longer, whereas words are always treated as a species of constituent.

[9]This conception of a lexicon is rather impoverished. In particular, it leaves out information about the meanings and uses of words, except what might be generally associated with the grammatical categories. While this impoverished conception is standard in the formal theory of CFG, attempts to use CFG to describe actual natural languages have had lexicons that also included semantic information. The lexicon we develop later will be much richer in structure.

and 'φ' stands for a regular expression formed from lexical and/or nonlexical categories; the arrow is to be interpreted as meaning, roughly, 'can consist of'. These rules are called 'phrase structure rules'.

The left-hand side of each rule specifies a phrase type (including the sentence as a type of phrase), and the right-hand side gives a possible pattern for that type of phrase. Because phrasal categories can appear on the right-hand sides of rules, it is possible to have phrases embedded within other phrases. This permits CFGs to express regularities that seem like accidents when only simple regular expressions are permitted.

A CFG normally has one or more phrasal categories that are designated as 'initial symbols'. These are the types of phrases that can stand alone as sentences in the language. Most simple CFGs have just one initial symbol, namely 'S'. Any string of words that can be derived from one of the initial symbols by means of a sequence of applications of the rules of the grammar is licensed (or, as linguists like to say, 'generated') by the grammar. The language a grammar generates is simply the collection of all of the sentences it generates.

2.3.1 An Example

Consider the following CFG. (We use 'D' for 'Determiner', which includes what we have up to now been calling 'articles'.)

(11) a. Rules:

      S → NP VP
      NP → (D) A* N PP*
      VP → V (NP) (PP)
      PP → P NP

    b. Lexicon:

      D: the, some
      A: big, brown, old
      N: birds, fleas, dog, hunter
      V: attack, ate, watched
      P: for, beside, with

This grammar generates infinitely many English sentences. Let us look in detail at how it generates one sentence: *The big brown dog with fleas watched the birds beside the hunter.* We start with the symbol S, for 'Sentence'. This must consist of the sequence NP VP, since the first rule is the only one with S on the left-hand side. The second rule allows a wide range of possibilities for the NP, one of which is D A A N PP. This PP must consist of a P followed by an NP, by the fourth rule, and the NP so introduced may consist of just an N. The third rule allows VP to consist of V NP PP, and this NP can consist of a D followed by an N. Lastly, the final PP again consists of a P followed by an NP, and this NP also consists of a D followed by an N. Putting these steps together the S may consist of the string D A A N P N V D N P D N, which can be converted into the desired sentence by inserting appropriate words in place of their lexical categories. All of this can be summarized in the following figure (called a 'tree diagram'):

(12)

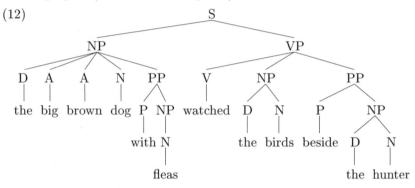

Note that certain sentences generated by this grammar can be associated with more than one tree. (Indeed, the example just given is one such sentence, but finding the other tree will be left as an exercise.) This illustrates how CFGs can overcome the second defect of regular expressions pointed out at the end of the previous section. Recall the ambiguity of (13):

(13) I saw the astronomer with a telescope.

The distinct interpretations of this sentence ('I used the telescope to see the astronomer'; 'What I saw was the astronomer who had a telescope') correspond to distinct tree structures that our grammar will assign to this string of words. The first interpretation corresponds to the tree where the PP *with a telescope* hangs from the VP; the latter is the meaning associated with the tree structure where that PP is part of the NP constituent: *the astronomer with a telescope*. CFG thus provides us with a straightforward mechanism for expressing such ambiguities, whereas grammars that use only regular expressions don't.

The normal way of talking about words and phrases is to say that certain word strings 'form a constituent'. What this means is that these strings function as units for some purpose (for example, the interpretation of modifiers) within the sentences in which they appear. So in (12), the sequence *with fleas* forms a PP constituent, *the big brown dog with fleas* forms an NP, and the sequence *dog with fleas* forms no constituent. Structural ambiguity arises whenever a string of words can form constituents in more than one way.

Problem 1: Practice with CFG

Assume the CFG grammar given in (11). Draw the tree structure for the other interpretation (i.e. not the one shown in (12)) of *The big brown dog with fleas watched the birds beside the hunter.*

⚠ Problem 2: More Practice with CFG

Assume the grammar rules given in (11), but with the following lexicon:

A: *big, unusual, young*
D: *a, the*
N: *cat, dog, hat, man, woman, roof*
P: *in, on, with*
V: *admired, disappeared, put, relied*

A. Give three sanctioned by this grammar that are well-formed English sentences. Draw the tree structures that the grammar assigns to them.

B. Give a well-formed English sentence that is structurally ambiguous according to this grammar. Draw the two distinct tree structures.

C. Give three sentences (using only the words from this grammar) that are not covered by this grammar but which are nonetheless well-formed in English. The examples should differ in their trees, not just in the lexical entries they contain.

D. Explain what prevents each of the examples in (C) from being covered.

E. Give three sentences sanctioned by this grammar that are not well-formed English sentences. Again, make them interestingly different.

F. Discuss how the grammar might be revised to correctly exclude your examples in (E), without simultaneously excluding good sentences.

G. How many sentences does this grammar admit?

H. How many would it admit if the NP rule were replaced by the following rule?

NP → (D) A N (PP) Explain your answer.

2.3.2 CFG as a Theory of Natural Language Grammar

As was the case with regular expressions, the formal properties of CFG are extremely well studied (see Hopcroft and Ullman (1979; chaps. 4–6) for a summary). In the early 1960s, several scholars published arguments purporting to show that natural languages exhibit properties beyond the descriptive capacity of CFGs. The pioneering work in the first two decades of generative grammar was based on the assumption that these arguments were sound. Most of that work can be viewed as the development of extensions to CFG designed to deal with the richness and complexity of natural languages.

The most celebrated proposed extension was a kind of rule called a 'transformation', as introduced into the field of generative grammar by Noam Chomsky.[10] Transformations are mappings from phrase structure representations to phrase structure representations (trees to trees, in our terms) that can copy, delete, and permute parts of trees, as well as insert specified new material into them. For example, in early work on transformations, it was claimed that declarative and interrogative sentence pairs (such as *The sun is shining* and *Is the sun shining?*) were to be derived from the same underlying phrase structure by a transformation that moved certain verbs to the front of the sentence. Likewise, passive sentences (such as *The cat was chased by the dog*) were derived from the same underlying structures as their active counterparts (*The dog chased the cat*) by means of a passivization transformation. The initial trees were to be generated by a CFG. The name 'transformational grammar' is sometimes used for theories positing rules of this sort.[11]

In 1982, the earlier arguments against the adequacy of CFG as a theory of natural language structure were called into question by Geoffrey Pullum and Gerald Gazdar. This led to a flurry of new work on the issue, culminating in new arguments that natural languages were not describable by CFGs. The mathematical and empirical work that resulted from this controversy substantially influenced the theory of grammar presented in this text. Many of the central papers in this debate were collected together by Savitch et al. (1987); of particular interest are Pullum and Gazdar's paper and Shieber's paper.

While the question of whether natural languages are in principle beyond the generative capacity of CFGs is of some intellectual interest, working linguists tend to be more concerned with determining what sort

---

[10]The original conception of a transformation, as developed in the early 1950s by Zellig Harris, was intended somewhat differently – as a way of regularizing the information content of texts, rather than as a system for generating sentences.

[11]See Appendix B for more discussion of varieties of transformational grammar.

of formalisms can provide elegant and enlightening accounts of linguistic phenomena in practice. Hence the arguments that tend to carry the most weight are ones about what formal devices are needed to capture linguistically significant generalizations. In the next chapter, we will consider some phenomena in English that suggest that the simple version of CFG introduced above should be extended.

2.3.3 Modern Phrase Structure Grammar

Accompanying the 1980s revival of interest in the mathematical properties of natural languages, considerable attention was given to the idea that, with an appropriately designed theory of syntactic features and general principles, context-free phrase structure grammar could serve as an empirically adequate theory of natural language syntax. This proposition was explored in great detail by Gazdar et al. (1985), who developed the theory known as 'Generalized Phrase Structure Grammar' (or GPSG). Work in phrase structure grammar advanced rapidly, and GPSG quickly evolved into a new framework, now known as 'Head-driven Phrase Structure Grammar' (HPSG), whose name reflects the increased importance of information encoded in the lexical heads[12] of syntactic phrases. The theory of grammar developed in this text is most closely related to current HPSG.

2.4 Applying Context-Free Grammar

In the previous sections, we introduced the formalism of context-free grammar and showed how it allows us to generate infinite collections of English sentences with simple rules. We also showed how it can provide a rather natural representation of certain ambiguities we find in natural languages. But the grammar we presented was just a teaching tool, designed to illustrate certain properties of the formalism; it was not intended to be taken seriously as an attempt to analyze the structure of English. In this section, we begin by motivating some phrase structure rules for English. In the course of doing this, we develop a new test for determining which strings of words are constituents. We also introduce a new abbreviatory convention that permits us to collapse many of our phrase structure rules into rule schemas.

2.4.1 Some Phrase Structure Rules for English

For the most part, we will use the traditional parts of speech, such as noun, verb, adjective, and preposition. In some cases, we will find it useful to introduce grammatical categories that might be new to readers, and we may apply the traditional labels somewhat differently than in

---

[12]The notion of 'head' will be discussed in section 2.7 below.

traditional grammar books. But the traditional classification of words into types has proved to be an extremely useful categorization over the past two millenia, and we see no reason to abandon it wholesale.

We turn now to phrases, beginning with noun phrases.

Noun Phrases

Nouns can appear in a number of positions, such as the positions of the three nouns in *Dogs give people fleas*. These same positions also allow sequences of an article followed by a noun, as in *The boy gave the dog a bath*. Since the position of the article can also be filled by demonstratives (e.g. *this, these*), possessives (e.g. *my, their*), or quantifiers (e.g. *each, some, many*), we use the more general term 'determiner' (abbreviated D) for this category. We can capture these facts by positing a type of phrase we'll call NP (for 'noun phrase'), and the rule NP → (D) N. As we saw earlier in this chapter, this rule will need to be elaborated later to include adjectives and other modifiers. First, however, we should consider a type of construction we have not yet discussed.

Coordination

To account for examples like *A dog, a cat, and a wombat fought*, we want a rule that allows sequences of NPs, with *and* before the last one, to appear where simple NPs can occur. A rule that does this is NP → NP$^+$ CONJ NP.

Whole sentences can also be conjoined, as in *The dog barked, the donkey brayed, and the pig squealed*. Again, we could posit a rule like S → S$^+$ CONJ S. But now we have two rules that look an awful lot alike. We can collapse them into one rule schema as follows, where the variable 'X' can be replaced by any grammatical category name:

(14) X → X$^+$ CONJ X.

Now we have made a claim that goes well beyond the data that motivated the rule, namely, that elements of any category can be conjoined in the same way. If this is correct, then we can use it as a test to see whether a particular string of words should be treated as a phrase. In fact, coordinate conjunction is widely used as a test for constituency. Though it is not an infallible diagnostic, we will use it as one of our sources of evidence for constituent structure.

Verb Phrases

Consider (15):

(15) The man yelled, chased the cat, and gave the dog a bone.

(15) contains the coordination of strings consisting of V, V NP, and
V NP NP. According to (14), this means that all three strings are constituents of the same type. Hence, we posit a constituent which we'll
call VP, described by the rule VP → V (NP) (NP). VP is introduced by
the rule S → NP VP.[13]

Prepositional Phrases

Expressions like *in Rome* or *at noon* that denote places or times ('locative' and 'temporal' expressions, as linguists would say) can be added
to almost any sentence, and to NPs, too. For example:

(16) a.   The fool yelled at noon.
     b.   This disease gave Leslie a fever in Rome.
     c.   A man in Rome laughed.

These are constituents, as indicated by examples like *The fool yelled
at noon and at midnight, in Rome and in Paris.* We can get lots of them
in one sentence, for example, *A man laughed on the street in Rome at
noon on Tuesday.* These facts can be incorporated into the grammar in
terms of the phrasal category PP (for 'prepositional phrase'), and the
rules:

(17) a.   PP → P NP
     b.   VP → VP PP

Since the second rule has VP on both the right and left sides of the arrow,
it can apply to its own output. (Such a rule is known as a RECURSIVE
rule).[14] Each time it applies, it adds a PP to the derivation. Thus, this
recursive rule permits arbitrary numbers of PPs within a VP.

As mentioned earlier, locative and temporal PPs can also occur in
NPs, for example, *A painter on the street in Rome on Tuesday at noon
laughed.* The most obvious analysis to try for this would be a rule that
said: NP → NP PP. However, we're going to adopt a slightly more
complex analysis. We posit a new nonlexical category, which we'll call
NOM, and we replace our old rule: NP → (D) N with the following:

---

[13]There are other kinds of coordinate sentences that we are leaving aside here – in
particular, elliptical sentences that involve coordination of nonconstituent sequences:

   (i) Chris likes blue and Pat green.
   (ii) Leslie wants to go home tomorrow, and Terry, too.

Notice that this kind of sentence, which will not be treated by the coordination rule
discussed in the text, has a characteristic intonation pattern – the elements after the
conjunction form separate intonational units separated by pauses.

[14]More generally, we use the term RECURSION whenever rules permit a constituent
to occur within a larger constituent of the same type.

(18) a. NP → (D) NOM
    b. NOM → N
    c. NOM → NOM PP

The category NOM will be very useful later in the text. For now, we will justify it with the following sentences:

(19) a. The love of my life and mother of my children would never do such a thing.
    b. The museum displayed no painting by Miro or drawing by Klee.

(19b) means that the museum displayed neither paintings by Miro nor drawings by Klee. That is, the determiner *no* must be understood as 'having scope' over both *painting by Miro* and *drawing by Klee* – it applies to both phrases. The most natural noun phrase structure to associate with this interpretation is:

(20) no [painting by Miro or drawing by Klee]

This, in turn, is possible with our current rules if the bracketed string is a conjoined NOM. It would not be possible without NOM.

Similarly, for (19a), *the* has scope over both *love of my life* and *mother of my children* and hence provides motivation for an analysis involving coordination of NOM constituents.

2.4.2 Summary of Grammar Rules

Our grammar now has the following rules:

(21)   S → NP VP
        NP → (D) NOM
        VP → V (NP) (NP)
        NOM → N
        NOM → NOM PP
        VP → VP PP
        PP → P NP
        X → X$^+$ CONJ X

In motivating this grammar, we encountered three types of arguments for saying a given string is a constituent:

- It exemplifies a pattern that shows up in multiple environments.
- Calling it a constituent helps us account for structural ambiguity.
- It can be a coordinate conjunct.

We will make use of all three of these types of arguments in the coming chapters.

2.5   Trees Revisited

In grouping words into phrases and smaller phrases into larger ones, we are assigning internal structure to sentences. As noted earlier, this structure can be represented in a tree diagram. For example, our grammar so far generates the following tree:

(22)

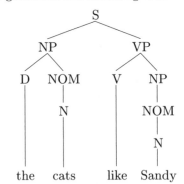

the   cats   like   Sandy

A tree is said to consist of NODES, connected by BRANCHES. A node above another on a branch is said to DOMINATE it. The nodes at the bottom of the tree – that is, those that do not dominate anything else – are referred to as TERMINAL nodes (or occasionally, as 'leaves'). A node right above another node on a tree is said to be its MOTHER and to IMMEDIATELY DOMINATE it. A node right below another on a branch is said to be its DAUGHTER. Two daughters of the same mother node are, naturally, referred to as SISTERS.

One way to think of the way in which a grammar of this kind defines (or generates) trees is as follows. First, we appeal to the lexicon (still conceived of as just a list of words paired with their grammatical categories) to tell us which lexical trees are well formed. (By 'lexical tree', we simply mean a tree consisting of a single nonterminal node dominating a single terminal node). So if *cats* is listed in the lexicon as belonging to the category N, and *like* is listed as a V, and so forth, then lexical structures like the following are well formed.

(23)

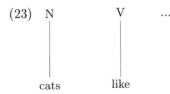

cats   like

And the grammar rules are equally straightforward. They simply tell us how well-formed trees (some of which may be lexical) can be combined into bigger ones:

(24)

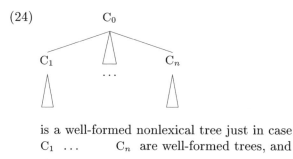

is a well-formed nonlexical tree just in case
C_1 ... C_n are well-formed trees, and

$C_0 \rightarrow C_1 ... C_n$ is a grammar rule.

So we can think of our grammar as generating sentences in a 'bottom-up' fashion – starting with lexical trees, and then using these to build bigger and bigger phrasal trees, until we build one whose top node is S. The set of all sentences that can be built that have S as their top node is the set of sentences the grammar generates. But note that our grammar could just as well have been used to generate sentences in a 'top-down' manner, starting with S. The set of sentences generated in this way is exactly the same. In fact, the definition of well-formed nonlexical tree could also be given in static, constraint-based terms as in (25):

(25) A tree is well formed just in case each local subtree (that is, a mother node with its daughters) within it either
1. is a well-formed lexical tree (see above), or
2. is in one-to-one (tree-to-rule) correspondence with some rule of the grammar.

A CFG is completely neutral with respect to top-down and bottom-up perspectives on analyzing sentence structure. There is also no particular bias toward thinking of the grammar in terms of generating sentences or in terms of parsing.

These design properties – direction neutrality and process neutrality – stem from the fact that the rules and lexical entries simply provide constraints on well-formed structure. As we will suggest in Chapter 9, these are in fact important design features of this theory (and of those we will develop that are based on it), as they facilitate the direct embedding of the abstract grammar within a model of language processing.

The lexicon and grammar rules together thus constitute a system for defining not only well-formed word strings (i.e. sentences), but also well-formed tree structures. Our statement of the relationship between the grammar rules and the well-formedness of trees is at present rather trivial, and our lexical entries still consist simply of pairings of words with parts of speech. As we modify our theory of grammar and enrich our lexicon, however, our attention will increasingly turn to a more refined characterization of which trees are well formed.

2.6 Worksection on Phrase Structure Grammar

Two of our arguments against overly simple theories of grammar at the beginning of this chapter were that we wanted to be able to account for the infinity of language, and that we wanted to be able to account for structural ambiguity. The purpose of this section is to explore how our grammar handles these so far.

Problem 3: Structural Ambiguity

Show that our grammar can account for the ambiguity of each of the following sentences by providing at least two trees licensed for each one, and explain briefly which interpretation goes with which tree:

   (i) Bo saw the group with the telescope.
   (ii) Most dogs and cats with fleas live in this neighborhood.
   (iii) The pictures show Superman and Lois Lane and Wonder Woman.

[*Note: We haven't provided a lexicon, so technically, our grammar doesn't generate any of these. You can assume, however, that all the words in them are in the lexicon, with the obvious category assignments.*]

Problem 4: Infinity

Our grammar has two mechanisms, each of which permits us to have infinitely many sentences: the Kleene operators (plus and star), and recursion (categories that can dominate themselves). Construct arguments for why we need both of them. That is, why not use recursion to account for the unboundedness of coordination or use Kleene star to account for the possibility of arbitrary numbers of PPs? [*Hint: Consider the different groupings into phrases – that is, the different tree structures – provided by the two mechanisms. Then look for English data supporting one choice of structure over another.*]

2.7 Heads

As we have seen, CFGs can provide successful analyses of quite a bit of natural language. But if our theory of natural language syntax were nothing more than CFG, our theory would fail to predict the fact that certain kinds of CF rules are much more natural than others. For example, consider the rules in (26):

(26) VP → P NP
     NP → PP S

As far as we are aware, no linguist has ever wanted to write rules like these for any human language. However, nothing in the formalism of CFG indicates that there is anything wrong – or even unusual – about such rules.

What is it that we don't like about the rules in (26)? An intuitive answer is that the categories on the left of the rules don't seem appropriate for the sequences on the right. For example, a VP should have a verb in it. This then leads us to consider why we named NP, VP, and PP after the lexical categories N, V, and P. In each case, the phrasal category was named after a lexical category that is an obligatory part of that kind of phrase. At least in the case of NP and VP, all other parts of the phrase may sometimes be missing (e.g. *Dogs bark*).

The lexical category that a phrasal category derives its name from is called the HEAD of the phrase. This notion of 'headedness' plays a crucial role in all human languages and this fact points out a way in which natural language grammars differ from some kinds of CFG. The formalism of CFG, in and of itself, treats category names as arbitrary: our choice of pairs like 'N' and 'NP', etc., serves only a mnemonic function in simple CFGs. But we want our theory to do more. Many phrase structures of natural languages are headed structures, a fact we will build into the architecture of our grammatical theory. To do this, we will enrich how we represent grammatical categories, so that we can express directly what a phrase and its head have in common. This will lead eventually to a dramatic reduction in the number of grammar rules required.

2.8 Subcategorization

The few grammar rules we have so far cover only a small fragment of English. What might not be so obvious, however, is that they also overgenerate – that is, they generate strings that are not well-formed English sentences. Both *denied* and *disappeared* would be listed in the lexicon as members of the category V. This classification is necessary to account for sentences like (27):

(27) a. The defendant denied the accusation.
     b. The problem disappeared.

But this would also permit the generation of the ungrammmatical sentences in (28).

(28)   a. *The defendant denied.
       b. *The teacher disappeared the problem.

Similarly, the verb *handed* must be followed by two NPs, but our rules allow a VP to be expanded in such a way that V can be followed by only one NP, or no NPs at all. That is, our current grammar fails to distinguish among the following:

(29)   a. The teacher handed the student a book.
       b. *The teacher handed the student.
       c. *The teacher handed a book.
       d. *The teacher handed.

To rule out the ungrammatical examples in (29), we need to distinguish among verbs that cannot be followed by an NP, those that must be followed by one NP, and those that must be followed by two NPs. These are often referred to as INTRANSITIVE, TRANSITIVE, and DITRANSITIVE verbs, respectively. In short, we need to distinguish subcategories of the category V.

One possible approach to this problem is simply to conclude that the traditional category of 'verb' is too coarse-grained for generative grammar, and that it must be replaced by at least three distinct categories, which we can call IV, TV, and DTV. We can then replace our earlier phrase structure rule

VP → V (NP) (NP)

with the following three rules:

(30)   a. VP → IV
       b. VP → TV NP
       c. VP → DTV NP NP

⚠ Problem 5: Properties Common to Verbs

This grammar embodies the claim that IVs, TVs, and DTVs are entirely different categories. Hence, it provides no reason to expect that they would have more in common than any other collection of three lexical categories, say, N, P, and D. But these three types of verbs do behave alike in a number of ways. For example, they all exhibit agreement with the subject of the sentence; this is discussed in the next section. List as many other properties as you can think of that are shared by intransitive, transitive, and ditransitive verbs.

2.9 Transitivity and Agreement

Most nouns and verbs in English have both singular and plural forms. In the case of nouns, the distinction between, say, *bird* and *birds* indicates whether the word is being used to refer to just one fowl or a multiplicity of them. In the case of verbs, distinctions like the one between *sing* and *sings* indicate whether the verb's subject denotes one or many individuals. In present tense English sentences, the plurality marking on the head noun of the subject NP and that on the verb must be consistent with each other. This is referred to as SUBJECT-VERB AGREEMENT (or sometimes just 'agreement' for short). It is illustrated in (31).

(31) a. The bird sings.
      b. Birds sing.
      c. *The bird sing.[15]
      d. *Birds sings.

Perhaps the most obvious strategy for dealing with agreement is the one considered in the previous section. That is, we could divide our grammatical categories into smaller categories, distinguishing singular and plural forms. We could then replace the relevant phrase structure rules with more specific ones. In examples like (31), we could distinguish lexical categories of N-SING and N-PLU, as well as IV-SING and IV-PLU. Then we could replace the rule

S → NP VP

with two rules:

S → NP-SING VP-SING

and

S → NP-PLU VP-PLU.

Since the marking for number appears on the head noun and head verb, other rules would also have to be changed. Specifically, the rules expanding NP and VP all would have to be divided into pairs of rules expanding NP-SING, NP-PLU, VP-SING, and VP-PLU. Hence, we would need all of the following:

(32) a. NP-SING → (D) NOM-SING
      b. NP-PLU → (D) NOM-PLU
      c. NOM-SING → NOM-SING PP
      d. NOM-PLU → NOM-PLU PP
      e. NOM-SING → N-SING

---

[15] There are dialects of English in which this is grammatical, but we will be analyzing the more standard dialect in which this kind of agreement marking is obligatory.

    f. NOM-PLU → N-PLU
    g. VP-SING → IV-SING
    h. VP-PLU → IV-PLU

This set of rules is cumbersome, and clearly misses linguistically significant generalizations. The rules in this set come in pairs, differing only in whether the category names end in '-SING' or '-PLU'. Nothing in the formalism or in the theory predicts this pairing. The rules would look no less natural if, for example, the rules expanding -PLU categories had their right-hand sides in the reverse order from those expanding -SING categories. But languages exhibiting this sort of variation in word order do not seem to exist.

Things get even messier when we consider transitive and ditransitive verbs. Agreement is required irrespective of whether the verb is intransitive, transitive, or ditransitive. Thus, along with (31), we have (33) and (34).

(33) a. The bird devours the worm.
      b. The birds devour the worm.
      c. *The bird devour the worm.
      d. *The birds devours the worm.

(34) a. The bird gives the worm a tug.
      b. The birds give the worm a tug.
      c. *The bird give the worm a tug.
      d. *The birds gives the worm a tug.

If agreement is to be handled by the rules in (35):

(35) a. S → NP-SING VP-SING
      b. S → NP-PLU VP-PLU

then we will now need to introduce lexical categories TV-SING, TV-PLU, DTV-SING, and DTV-PLU, along with the necessary VP-SING and VP-PLU expansion rules (as well as the two rules in (35)). What are the rules for VP-SING and VP-PLU when the verb is transitive or ditransitive? For simplicity, we will look only at the case of VP-SING with a transitive verb. Since the object of the verb can be either singular or plural, we need two rules:

(36) a. VP-SING → TV-SING NP-SING
      b. VP-SING → TV-SING NP-PLU

Similarly, we need two rules for expanding VP-PLU when the verb is transitive, and four rules each for expanding VP-SING and VP-PLU when the verb is ditransitive (since each object can be either singular or plural). Alternatively, we could make all objects of category NP and introduce the following two rules:

(37) a. NP → NP-SING
      b. NP → NP-PLU

This would keep the number of VP-SING and VP-PLU rules down to three each (rather than seven each), but it introduces extra noun phrase categories. Either way, the rules are full of undesirable redundancy.

⚠ Problem 6: Pronoun Case

There are some differences between the noun phrases that can appear in different positions. In particular, pronouns in subject position have one form (referred to as NOMINATIVE, and including the pronouns *I, he, she, we,* and *they*), whereas pronouns in other positions take another form (called ACCUSATIVE, and including *me, him, her, us,* and *them*). So, for example, we say *He saw her,* not **Him saw she.*

  a. How would the category of NP have to be further subdivided in order to account for the difference between nominative and accusative pronouns?

  b. How would the rules for S and the various kinds of VPs have to be modified in order to account for the distributional differences between nominative and accusative pronouns?

It should be clear by now that as additional coverage is incorporated – such as adjectives modifying nouns – the redundancies will proliferate. The problem is that we want to be able to talk about nouns and verbs as general classes, but we have now divided nouns into (at least) two categories (N-SING and N-PLU) and verbs into six categories (IV-SING, IV-PLU, TV-SING, TV-PLU, DTV-SING, and DTV-PLU). To make agreement work, this multiplication of categories has to be propagated up through at least some of the phrasal categories. The result is a very long and repetitive list of phrase structure rules.

What we need is a way to talk about subclasses of categories, without giving up the commonality of the original categories. That is, we need a formalism that permits us to refer straightforwardly to, for example, all verbs, all singular verbs, all ditransitive verbs, or all singular ditransitive verbs. In the next chapter, we introduce a device that will permit us to do this.

2.10 Conclusion

In this chapter, we began our search for an adequate model of the grammar of one natural language: English. We considered and rejected two simple approaches to grammar, including a theory based on regular expressions ('finite-state grammar'). The theory of Context-Free Grammars, by contrast, solves the obvious defects of these simple approaches and provides an appropriate starting point for the grammatical description of natural language. However, we isolated two ways in which Context-Free Grammars are inadequate as a theory of natural language:

- CFGs are arbitrary. They fail to predict the 'headedness' that is characteristic of many types of phrase in natural language.
- CFGs are redundant. Without some way to refer to kinds of categories rather than just individual categories, there is no way to eliminate the massive redundancy that will be required in order to analyze the agreement patterns of natural languages.

For these reasons, we cannot accept CFG alone as a theory of grammar. As we will show in the next few chapters, however, it is possible to retain much of the character of CFG as we seek to remedy its defects.

2.11 Further Reading

The standard reference work for the basic mathematical results on formal languages (including regular expressions and context-free languages) is Hopcroft and Ullman (1979). Partee et al. (1990) covers much of the same material from a more linguistic perspective. Classic works arguing against the use of context-free grammars for natural languages include Chomsky (1963) and Postal (1964). Papers questioning these arguments, and other papers presenting new arguments for the same conclusion are collected in Savitch et al. (1987). For (somewhat dated) surveys of theories of grammar, see Sells (1985) and Wasow (1989). A more detailed presentation of GPSG is Gazdar et al. (1985). The history of generative grammar is presented from different perspectives by Matthews (1993), Newmeyer (1986), Harris (1993), and Huck and Goldsmith (1995).

Perhaps the best discussions of the basic phrase structures of English are to be found in good descriptive grammars, such as Quirk et al. (1972, 1985) or Greenbaum (1996). Important discussions of the notion of 'head' and its role in phrase structure can be found in Chomsky (1970) and Gazdar and Pullum (1981). A detailed taxonomy of the subcategories of English verbs is provided by Levin (1993).

3

Analyzing Features of Grammatical Categories

3.1 Introduction

In the last chapter, we saw that there are constraints on which words can go together (what linguists call 'co-occurrence restrictions') that are not efficiently described using the standard formalism of context-free grammar. Some verbs must take an object; others can never take an object; still others (e.g. *put, inform*) require both an object and another phrase of a particular kind. These co-occurrence restrictions, as we have seen, give rise to a great deal of redundancy in CFGs. In addition, different forms of a given verb impose different conditions on what kind of NP can precede them (i.e. on what kind of subject they co-occur with). For example, *walks* requires a third-person singular NP as its subject; *walk* requires a plural subject, or else one that is first- or second-person singular. As we saw in the last chapter, if we try to deal with this complex array of data by dividing the category V into more specific categories, each with its unique co-occurrence restrictions, we end up with a massively redundant grammar that fails to capture linguistically significant generalizations.

We also isolated a second defect of CFGs, namely that they allow rules that are arbitrary. Nothing in the theory of CFG reflects the fact that the phrases of human language usually share certain key properties (nounhood, verbhood, prepositionhood, etc.) with a particular daughter within them – their head. We must somehow modify the theory of CFG to allow us to express the property of headedness.

Our solution to the problem of redundancy is to make grammatical categories decomposable into component parts. CFG as presented so far treats each grammatical category symbol as atomic – that is, without internal structure. Two categories are either identical or different; there

47

is no mechanism for saying that two categories are alike in some ways, but different in others. However, words and phrases in natural languages typically behave alike in certain respects, but not in others. For example, the two words *deny* and *denies* are alike in requiring an NP object (both being forms of a transitive verb). But they differ in terms of the kind of subject NP they take: *denies* requires a third-person-singular subject like *Kim* or *she*, while *deny* accepts most any NP subject except the third-person-singular kind. On the other hand, *denies* and *disappears* both take a singular subject NP, but only the former can co-occur with a following object NP. An adequate formalism needs to be able to characterize the fact that words are organized into classes defined in terms of cross-cutting properties.

To accommodate this intuition, we will develop the view that grammatical categories are not atomic, but rather are complexes with internal structure. This innovation, much like the decomposition of molecules into atoms, or of atoms into subatomic particles, will allow us to talk precisely about how categories are the same in certain respects, yet different in others.

3.2 Feature Structures

Informally, we speak of verbs differing in their transitivity. More generally, linguists talk about elements that have different combinatoric potential in terms of differing 'valence'.[1] Likewise, we talk of the number (singular or plural) of a noun, the part of speech of a word (whether it's a noun, verb, etc.), or a verb's form (e.g. whether it is a present participle, an infinitive, etc.). Instead of associating words in the lexicon with a single atomic category, we can treat a lexical category as a complex of grammatical properties. To model such complexes, we use the notion standardly referred to as FEATURE STRUCTURE.

A feature structure is a way of representing grammatical information. Formally, a feature structure consists of a specification of a set of features (which we will write in upper case), each of which is paired with a particular value. Feature structures can be thought of in at least two more or less equivalent ways. For example, they may be conceived of as functions (in the mathematicians' sense of the word)[2] specifying a value for each of a set of features, or else as directed graphs where feature names label arcs that point to appropriately labeled nodes. For

---

[1] This term, borrowed from chemistry, refers to the capacity to combine with atoms, ions, and the like.

[2] A function in this sense is a set of ordered pairs such that no two ordered pairs in the set share the same first element. What this means for feature structures is that each feature in a feature structure must have a unique value.

grammatical purposes, however, it will be most useful for us to focus on DESCRIPTIONS of feature structures, which we will write in a square bracket notation, as shown in (1):

$$(1) \quad \begin{bmatrix} \text{FEATURE}_1 & \text{VALUE}_1 \\ \text{FEATURE}_2 & \text{VALUE}_2 \\ \cdots & \\ \text{FEATURE}_n & \text{VALUE}_n \end{bmatrix}$$

For example, we might treat the category of the word *bird* in terms of a feature structure that specifies both part of speech and number. We may assume such a category includes appropriate specifications for two appropriately named features: its part of speech (POS) is noun, and its number (NUM) is singular (sg). The lexical entry for *bird*, then, would be a pair consisting of a form and a feature structure description, roughly as shown in (2):[3]

$$(2) \quad \left\langle \text{bird,} \begin{bmatrix} \text{POS} & \text{noun} \\ \text{NUM} & \text{sg} \end{bmatrix} \right\rangle$$

Implicit in our use of feature structures is a commitment to developing a theory of what kinds of features go together, what values are appropriate for each particular feature, etc. – that is, a commitment to specifying which feature structure categories are well formed and which are not. Note that this enterprise is also naturally viewed as providing a theory of what kind of linguistic entities exist in a given domain, and what properties those entities exhibit. Much of our grammar development will be concerned with formulating a natural theory of linguistic generalizations in terms of the constraints that govern the feature structure categories we are led to posit.

One of the first things we will want to do in developing a theory of grammar is to classify linguistic entities in various ways. To this end, it is particularly useful to introduce the notion of TYPE. This concept is really quite simple: if we think of a language as a system of linguistic entities (words, phrases, categories, sounds, and other more abstract entities that we will introduce as we go along), then types are just classes of those entities. We assign entities to these classes on the basis of certain properties that they share. Naturally, the properties we employ in our type classification will be those that we wish to refer to

---

[3]Throughout this book, we will describe linguistic forms in terms of standard English orthography. In fact, a lexical entry such as this should contain a phonological description that will play a role in the word's phonological realization, a topic we will not consider in detail here.

in our descriptions of the entities. Thus each grammatical type will be associated with particular features and sometimes with particular values for those features.

Let us make this very abstract discussion more concrete by considering the use of feature structures to describe a simple nonlinguistic domain. Imagine that we used feature structures to model universities and the people who are associated with them. We'll start from the assumption that the people and the other entities are really 'out there' in the real world. Our first step then in constructing a theory of this part of the world is to develop a model. A simple model will be a set of mathematical entities that we assume to correspond to the real ones. Our theory will be successful to the extent that we can show that the properties that our theory ascribes to our modeling entities (through stipulation or deduction from the stipulations) also hold of the real world entities they are assumed to correspond to.

The most general kind of entity in the domain at hand should include universities, departments, and individuals (people). We might want to talk about certain properties of these entities, for example their name or telephone number. In this case, we would declare the existence of a general type called *entity* and say that the features NAME and TEL(EPHONE) are appropriate features for all entities (tokens) of this type. So for each university, department, or person in this university world, we would hypothesize a distinct feature structure model that we could describe as follows:

(3) a. $\begin{bmatrix} \textit{entity} \\ \text{NAME} \quad \text{Stanford University} \\ \text{TEL} \quad\quad 650\text{-}723\text{-}2300 \end{bmatrix}$

   b. $\begin{bmatrix} \textit{entity} \\ \text{NAME} \quad \text{Gerhard Casper} \\ \text{TEL} \quad\quad 650\text{-}723\text{-}2481 \end{bmatrix}$

   c. $\begin{bmatrix} \textit{entity} \\ \text{NAME} \quad \text{Stanford Linguistics} \\ \text{TEL} \quad\quad 650\text{-}723\text{-}4284 \end{bmatrix}$

Note that we use type names, written in italics, as labels on the top line within feature structures.

Of course 'entity' is a very general classification – our theory would not have progressed far if it recognized no more specific kinds of things. So in fact, we would want our theory to include the fact that there are different subtypes of the type *entity*. Let's call these new types *university*, *department*, and *individual*. Entities belonging to each of these types have their own special properties. For example, individual people have birthdays, but universities and departments don't (or not in the same sense). Similarly, departments have chairs (or 'heads of department'), but neither universities nor individuals do. Finally, only universities have presidents. We can accommodate these facts by declaring each of the relevant features (BIRTHDAY, CHAIR, PRESIDENT) to be appropriate for the right one of our new subtypes. This formal declaration is just a precise way of saying that the members of the relevant subclasses have certain properties that distinguish them from other entities in the system. The resulting descriptions that we write will be appropriately more specific, as in (4):

(4) a.
$$\begin{bmatrix} \textit{university} \\ \text{NAME} \quad\quad \text{Stanford University} \\ \text{PRESIDENT} \quad \text{Gerhard Casper} \\ \text{TEL} \quad\quad\quad \text{650-723-2300} \end{bmatrix}$$

   b.
$$\begin{bmatrix} \textit{individual} \\ \text{NAME} \quad\quad \text{Gerhard Casper} \\ \text{BIRTHDAY} \quad \text{12-25-1937} \\ \text{TEL} \quad\quad\quad \text{650-723-2481} \end{bmatrix}$$

   c.
$$\begin{bmatrix} \textit{department} \\ \text{NAME} \quad\quad \text{Stanford Linguistics} \\ \text{CHAIR} \quad\quad \text{Stanley Peters} \\ \text{TEL} \quad\quad\quad \text{650-723-4284} \end{bmatrix}$$

Note that each of these descriptions reflects the hierarchical organization of types. Each type of entity has its own constellation of features – some of them were declared appropriate for the indicated subtype; others were sanctioned by the supertype *entity*. This is a simple illustration of how a hierarchical classification system works. A given feature structure contains only those features that are declared appropriate by one of its types, that is, by its LEAF type[4] or one of its supertypes. As we will see, a feature structure also inherits any type constraints, (that is, constraints on feature values) that are associated with its supertypes. Articulating a type hierarchy and the feature structures associated with each type is an important component of a theory that uses typed feature structures as models.

---

[4]The leaf types are the basic or bottom-level types in a hierarchy, i.e. the types that have no subtypes. These are often referred to in the literature (somewhat counterintuitively) as 'maximal' types.

To talk about merging information from more than one source, that is, when we know that two feature structure descriptions describe the same entity, we're going to need a precise method for combining these descriptions. A standard method for doing this is called UNIFICATION. Unification corresponds intuitively to the notion of identity that we have already used, indicated by two occurrences of a single variable (e.g. the category variable 'X' used in our coordination rule) to refer to a single entity (e.g. a particular grammatical category like NP or S in particular instantiations of the coordination schema). Up to now, we have used these identities only for atomic values. Once we recognize feature structures as entities, however, we can think of each description as being satisfied by some set of feature structures. A feature structure description can thus be partial (satisfied by many distinct feature structures) or total (being satisfied by only one). Any such description must be consistent, precisely because it specifies a set of objects (those that satisfy the description).

Unification, then, is just a general method for allowing two compatible descriptions to amalgamate the information they contain into a single (usually larger) description. Since all descriptions must be consistent, it follows that two feature structure descriptions can unify only if they are consistent – that is, unless they specify conflicting types or different atomic values for the same feature. The unification of two feature structure descriptions is just the description obtained by combining all of the information from both of them. If D_1 is satisfied by a set (of feature structures) σ_1 and D_2 is satisfied by a set σ_2, then the unification of D_1 and D_2 (written $D_1 \sqcup D_2$) is satisfied by the intersection of σ_1 and σ_2.

For example, the feature structure descriptions in (5) cannot unify

(5) a. $\begin{bmatrix} university \\ \text{NAME} & \text{Stanford University} \end{bmatrix}$

    b. $\begin{bmatrix} university \\ \text{NAME} & \text{Harvard University} \end{bmatrix}$

because they differ in the value they assign to the feature NAME. Intuitively, these two descriptions cannot describe the same entity. Similarly, the descriptions in (6) cannot unify

(6) a. $\begin{bmatrix} individual \\ \text{TEL} & \text{650-555-4284} \end{bmatrix}$

    b. $\begin{bmatrix} department \\ \text{TEL} & \text{650-555-4284} \end{bmatrix}$

because they specify incompatible types, namely, *individual* and *department*, and hence cannot describe the same entity. But the feature structure description in (7) unifies with any of those in (8a)–(8c).

(7) $\begin{bmatrix} \text{TEL} & \text{910-234-5789} \end{bmatrix}$

(8) a. $\begin{bmatrix} \textit{university} \end{bmatrix}$

   b. $\begin{bmatrix} \textit{individual} \\ \text{NAME} \quad \text{Xena: Warrior Princess} \end{bmatrix}$

   c. $\begin{bmatrix} \textit{department} \\ \text{NAME} \quad \text{Metaphysics} \\ \text{CHAIR} \quad \text{Alexius Meinong, Jr.} \end{bmatrix}$

In each case, the result of unification is the description containing the information from each of the two descriptions unified, and nothing more. Thus the unification of (7) and (8b) is (9):

(9) $\begin{bmatrix} \textit{individual} \\ \text{NAME} \quad \text{Xena: Warrior Princess} \\ \text{TEL} \quad \text{910-234-5789} \end{bmatrix}$

We will often use unification to indicate that two different feature structures in fact have the same value for a given feature. To take a simple example, we might want to indicate that two different departments have the same phone number in the world we are describing. We will indicate this by two identical occurrences of a given boxed integer, or 'tag', as illustrated in (10).

(10) $\begin{bmatrix} \textit{department} \\ \text{NAME} \quad \text{Metaphysics} \\ \text{TEL} \quad \boxed{2} \end{bmatrix} \begin{bmatrix} \textit{department} \\ \text{NAME} \quad \text{Philosophy} \\ \text{TEL} \quad \boxed{2} \end{bmatrix}$

And of course we might want to simultaneously indicate a feature identity and the value of the feature, as shown in (11):

(11) $\begin{bmatrix} \textit{department} \\ \text{NAME} \quad \text{Metaphysics} \\ \text{TEL} \quad \boxed{2}\text{800-374-6786} \end{bmatrix} \begin{bmatrix} \textit{department} \\ \text{NAME} \quad \text{Philosophy} \\ \text{TEL} \quad \boxed{2} \end{bmatrix}$

Note that it would make no difference if we wrote the phone number after the other occurrence of $\boxed{2}$ in (11). The intended interpretation would be exactly the same. It also makes no difference what order we write the features in. So (11) is equivalent, for example, to the following:

(12) $\begin{bmatrix} department \\ \text{TEL} \qquad \boxed{2}\text{800-374-6786} \\ \text{NAME} \qquad \text{Philosophy} \end{bmatrix}$ $\begin{bmatrix} department \\ \text{NAME} \qquad \text{Metaphysics} \\ \text{TEL} \qquad \boxed{2} \end{bmatrix}$

Since the value of the feature TEL is atomic (i.e. it can bear no feature specifications of its own), the unification of values of this feature is much like the simple identity we expressed in the previous chapter by means of multiple occurrences of a variable (e.g. the variable X in the coordination schema). But in the chapters that follow, we will have occasion to unify feature structure descriptions that are embedded as the value of some feature.

3.3 The Linguistic Application of Feature Structures

3.3.1 Feature Structure Categories

So how do feature structures help us with our linguistic deliberations? Instead of saying that there is just one kind of linguistic entity, which must bear a value for every feature we recognize in our feature structures, we will often want to say that a given entity is of a certain type and that certain features are appropriate only for things of that type. We will use typing in many ways, to ensure that [NUM sg] (or [NUM pl]) can only be specified for certain kinds of words (nouns and pronouns, for example), but not, for instance, for prepositions or adjectives.[5] Likewise, we will eventually want to distinguish auxiliaries (helping verbs like *will* and *have*) from other kinds of verbs in terms of a feature AUX. However, we will not want to say that nouns are all redundantly specified as [AUX –], but rather that the feature AUX just isn't appropriate for nouns. We can use types as a basis for classifying the feature structures we assume and the constraints we use to describe them. In so doing, we can then simply state that particular features only go with certain types of feature structures. This amounts to the beginnings of a linguistic ontology – that is, the types tell us what kind of linguistic entities exist, according to our theory, and the features associated with those types tell us what general properties those entities exhibit. In this way, we also make feature structures compact, that is, we make them reflect only information that is appropriate for the kind of linguistic entity they are associated with.

The hierarchical organization of linguistic types in our theory is significant. As illustrated above, this enables us to classify feature struc-

---

[5]Many such restrictions are language-particular. For example, adjectives are distinguished according to number (agreeing with the noun they modify) in many languages. Even prepositions exhibit agreement inflection in some languages (e.g. modern Irish) and need to be classified in similar terms.

tures in more subtle ways that will allow intermediate level categories of various sorts. For example, verbs may be classified as intransitive or transitive; and transitive verbs may then be further subclassified as strict transitive (those taking a direct object and nothing else) or ditransitive. A hierarchical type system will let us talk about the properties shared by two distinct types (e.g. strict transitive and ditransitive) by associating a feature or a constraint with their common supertype (transitive).

To start, let us draw a very intuitive type distinction – between *word* and *phrase*. Our grammar rules (i.e. our phrase structure rules) all specify the properties of phrases; the lexicon provides a theory of words. Continuing our practice of indicating types as labels on feature structures, we will replace (2) above with (13):

(13)
$$\left\langle \text{ bird },\ \begin{bmatrix} word \\ \text{POS} & \text{noun} \\ \text{NUM} & \text{sg} \end{bmatrix} \right\rangle$$

We will now reformulate our grammar in terms of typed feature structures. We do so in two stages: first, we introduce the feature VAL (for 'valence'), without worrying about agreement. Then we present our first feature-based treatment of subject-verb agreement. Both of these analyses will be refined in subsequent chapters.

3.3.2 Representing Valence with a Feature

We can identify our earlier categories IV, TV, and DTV with the following three feature structures:

(14)
$$\text{IV} = \begin{bmatrix} word \\ \text{POS} & \text{verb} \\ \text{VAL} & \text{itr} \end{bmatrix} \quad \text{TV} = \begin{bmatrix} word \\ \text{POS} & \text{verb} \\ \text{VAL} & \text{tr} \end{bmatrix}$$

$$\text{DTV} = \begin{bmatrix} word \\ \text{POS} & \text{verb} \\ \text{VAL} & \text{dtr} \end{bmatrix}$$

These three categories all share the type *word* and the feature specification [POS verb]. This is just the combination of types and features that we would naturally identify with the category V. That is, by analyzing categories in terms of types and features, we can distinguish between the different valence possibilities for verbs, while still recognizing that all verbs fall under a general category. We can represent the general category by leaving the value of the VAL feature unspecified, as follows:

(15)
$$V = \begin{bmatrix} word \\ POS \quad verb \end{bmatrix}$$

The commonly used term in linguistics for leaving out feature specifications in order to specify a larger class of linguistic entities is UNDER-SPECIFICATION.

The category VP differs from the category V only with respect to its type assignment. So the feature structure for VP is the following:

(16)
$$VP = \begin{bmatrix} phrase \\ POS \quad verb \end{bmatrix}$$

And if we wanted to refer to the class that includes just verbs and verb phrases, we would refer to it as the underspecification in (17):

(17)
$$\begin{bmatrix} POS \quad verb \end{bmatrix}$$

Similarly, we can analyze the categories N and NP as follows:

(18)
$$N = \begin{bmatrix} word \\ POS \quad noun \end{bmatrix} \quad NP = \begin{bmatrix} phrase \\ POS \quad noun \end{bmatrix}$$

Our method of analysis in fact allows underspecification of various kinds. Our goal is to provide compact descriptions for those categories that our grammar will actually need to refer to, what linguists usually call 'natural classes'.

We will continue to use labels like V, N, VP, and NP, but they should now be regarded as abbreviations for the typed feature structures just described. Notice that the feature analysis we have just sketched does not accommodate the category NOM: since there are only two syntactic types, this system does not permit the sort of three-level phrases we posited for NPs in the previous chapter. In the next chapter, we will revise our treatment of the internal structure of categories in such a way that NOM can be distinguished both from N and from NP.

Turning now to the phrase structure rules, we can reformulate our VP rules in terms of our new feature structure categories. Consider the following way of stating these rules:

(19)
$$\begin{bmatrix} phrase \\ POS \quad \boxed{1} \end{bmatrix} \rightarrow \begin{bmatrix} word \\ POS \quad \boxed{1} \\ VAL \quad itr \end{bmatrix}$$

$$\begin{bmatrix} phrase \\ POS \quad \boxed{1} \end{bmatrix} \rightarrow \begin{bmatrix} word \\ POS \quad \boxed{1} \\ VAL \quad tr \end{bmatrix} NP$$

$$\begin{bmatrix} phrase \\ POS \quad \boxed{1} \end{bmatrix} \rightarrow \begin{bmatrix} word \\ POS \quad \boxed{1} \\ VAL \quad dtr \end{bmatrix} \text{NP NP}$$

The two occurrences of $\boxed{1}$ in each of these rules tell us that the POS value of the mother and that of the first daughter must be unified (which amounts to simple identity of atomic values in this case). Since the rules in (19) were introduced as VP rules, the obvious value to assign to $\boxed{1}$ is 'verb'. But by stating the rules in this underspecified way, we can use them to cover some other structures as well. The first rule, for intransitives, can be used to introduce nouns, which can never be sisters to NPs. This is done simply by instantiating $\boxed{1}$ as 'noun', which will in turn cause the mother to be an NP. To make this work right, we will have to specify that lexical nouns, like intransitive verbs, must be [VAL itr]. Similarly, the second rule can subsume our PP expansion rule, if $\boxed{1}$ is instantiated as 'prep' and prepositions are lexically marked [VAL tr], thus allowing PPs to be built from a preposition and an NP object.

We would also like to use underspecification to collapse into one the two recursive rules introducing PPs, that is, the rules VP $\rightarrow$ VP PP and NOM $\rightarrow$ NOM PP. At this point, we can't do so, because we haven't yet integrated NOM into our system of types and features. But we would like eventually to be able to replace these two rules with something like the following:[6]

(20) $\quad \begin{bmatrix} phrase \\ POS \quad \boxed{2} \end{bmatrix} \rightarrow \begin{bmatrix} phrase \\ POS \quad \boxed{2} \end{bmatrix} \text{PP}[\ldots]$

⚠ Problem 1: Other Uses for Rule (20)

The rule for PP modifiers given in (20) interacts with the coordination rule presented in the previous chapter. The coordination rule, as you may recall, is the following (with the 'X's of Chapter 2 now replaced by the more general tag notation):

$\boxed{1} \rightarrow \boxed{1}^+ \text{ CONJ } \boxed{1}$

In particular, the interaction of these rules predicts that a PP can modify a coordinate structure, as in examples like:

(i) Kim walks and reads books without difficulty
(ii) the poetry and the music on the program.

---

[6]Note that the choice of a particular tag here is entirely arbitrary – all that is crucial is that there be two occurrences of the same tag.

For the purposes of this problem, assume the following grammar, which we will refer to as $\mathbf{G_1}$.

Rules of $\mathbf{G_1}$:

$$\begin{bmatrix} phrase \\ \text{POS} \quad \boxed{2} \end{bmatrix} \rightarrow \begin{bmatrix} phrase \\ \text{POS} \quad \boxed{2} \end{bmatrix} \text{PP}[\ldots]$$

$$\boxed{1} \rightarrow \boxed{1}^{+} \quad \text{CONJ} \quad \boxed{1}$$

$$\text{S} \rightarrow \text{NP VP}$$

$$\text{NP} \rightarrow \text{(D) N}$$

$$\begin{bmatrix} phrase \\ \text{POS} \quad \boxed{1} \end{bmatrix} \rightarrow \begin{bmatrix} word \\ \text{POS} \quad \boxed{1} \\ \text{VAL} \quad itr \end{bmatrix}$$

$$\begin{bmatrix} phrase \\ \text{POS} \quad \boxed{1} \end{bmatrix} \rightarrow \begin{bmatrix} word \\ \text{POS} \quad \boxed{1} \\ \text{VAL} \quad tr \end{bmatrix} \text{NP}$$

$$\begin{bmatrix} phrase \\ \text{POS} \quad \boxed{1} \end{bmatrix} \rightarrow \begin{bmatrix} word \\ \text{POS} \quad \boxed{1} \\ \text{VAL} \quad dtr \end{bmatrix} \text{NP NP}$$

Sample Lexical Entries of $\mathbf{G_1}$:

$$\left\langle \text{bird} , \begin{bmatrix} word \\ \text{POS} \quad \text{noun} \\ \text{NUM} \quad \text{sg} \\ \text{VAL} \quad itr \end{bmatrix} \right\rangle$$

$$\left\langle \text{flies} , \begin{bmatrix} word \\ \text{POS} \quad \text{verb} \\ \text{VAL} \quad itr \end{bmatrix} \right\rangle$$

A. Draw the tree structure defined by $\mathbf{G_1}$ for (i) and (ii). Make sure the PP modifies the entire coordinate structure.

B. Draw a distinct tree structure defined by $\mathbf{G_1}$ for each of these same examples, but make sure that the PP does not modify the entire coordinate structure.

The new version of the PP modifier rule also predicts that other categories besides VP and NP can occur with PP modifiers.

C. Using coordination as part of your argument, construct crucial examples demonstrating that S can also co-occur with PP modifiers.

D. Find at least one more category that can be modified by a PP, providing examples to support your claim. (Note: You may consider types of phrases we have not yet discussed, as well as ones that have appeared in our rules.)

In the next chapter, we will carry even further the collapsing of phrase structure rules across POS values, when we revise our analysis of the valence feature. First, however, let us examine how features might be employed in the analysis of subject-verb agreement.

3.3.3 Representing Agreement with Features

One device introduced in the last section lends itself well to dealing with the problem of agreement. This is the use of a tag linking two feature values, the effect of which is to force two distinct nodes in a tree admitted by a rule to have identical values for a given feature. We can also employ this device to handle agreement by tagging values for the feature NUM. In the rule expanding S, we could require that the NP and the VP both have the same value of NUM, and we could use the same technique to ensure that the NUM value of a given phrase is identical to the NUM value of the lexical head of that phrase. With these revisions, the rules in question look like (21).

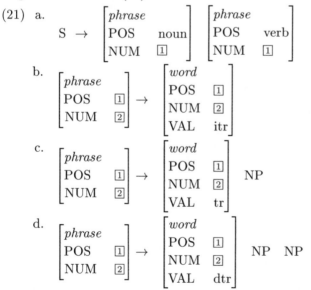

3.4 The Head Feature Principle

The last three rules in (21) require that the mother and one of the daughters bear identical (unified) values both for POS and for NUM. In fact, the constituent on the right-hand side that carries the matching feature values is always the head daughter. As we will see in later chapters, there are a number of properties of phrases that are also properties of their lexical heads.[7] In this section, we will develop general mechanisms for capturing the generalization that certain properties are characteristically shared by phrases and their heads.

Rather than stipulating identity of features in an ad hoc manner on both sides of the rules (as in (21)), our analysis will recognize that in a certain type of phrase – a HEADED PHRASE – one daughter is assigned special status as the HEAD DAUGHTER. Once such a notion is incorporated into our theory (thus providing a remedy for the second defect of standard CFGs noted in the last chapter), we can factor out the identity constraint that we need for all the headed phrases, making it a general principle. We will call this generalization the Head Feature Principle (HFP).

Certain rules, such as those in (21), introduce an element that functions as the head of the phrase characterized by the rule. We will call such rules HEADED RULES. To indicate which element introduced in a headed rule is the head daughter, we will label one element on the right hand side of the rule with the letter 'H'. So a headed rule will have the following general form:

(22)   [*phrase*] → ...   H[ ]   ...

Our goal is to formulate a general theory of what features the head daughter shares with its mother in a headed phrase, that is, what features will always be the same for the element labeled 'H' in a headed rule and the phrase licensed by the rule.[8]

Before proceeding, we need to reflect for a moment on parts of speech. As we noted above, there are certain features that are appropriate for certain parts of speech, but not others. For example, CASE is appropri-

---

[7]Alternative formulations might be that some properties of lexical heads are inherited by the phrases they 'project' or that properties of phrases are marked on the lexical heads. While it is often helpful to think of information as propagating up or down through a tree, this is just a metaphor. Our formulation of the generalization in the text avoids attributing directionality of causation in the sharing of properties between phrases and their heads.

[8]Note that 'H', unlike the other shorthand symbols we will use occasionally (e.g. 'V', 'NP'), does not abbreviate a feature structure in a grammar rule. Rather, it merely indicates which feature structure in the rule corresponds to the phrase's head daughter.

ate only for nouns (in English), while the feature AUX is specifiable only for verbs (to distinguish helping verbs from all others). Likewise, here we will use the features PER(SON) and NUM(BER) only for nouns, verbs, and determiners.[9] To guarantee that only the right features go with the right parts of speech, we will treat parts of speech not as atomic values of the POS feature, but rather in terms of a set of types.[10] Then we can declare which features are appropriate for each part of speech type.

We therefore introduce the types *noun, verb, adj, prep, det,* and *conj* for the six lexical categories we have so far considered. We then make all of these subtypes of a type called *part-of-speech (pos)*. Our grammar must also specify the appropriate values for each feature it employs. We will make the traditional assumption throughout this book that NUM takes either 'sg' (singular) or 'pl' (plural) as its value and that the values of PER are '1st', '2nd', or '3rd'.

Having eliminated the old feature POS, we now introduce a new one called HEAD. HEAD will always take as its value a part of speech, that is, a feature structure assigned to some subtype of the type *pos*. In this way, HEAD does the work formerly assigned to POS; but it also does more, namely, it provides a way for us to begin to provide an account of which features are appropriate for which parts of speech.

In making this change, it should be noted that we have also introduced a significant innovation into our theory of feature structures. Previously, all of our features' values were atoms (e.g. 'itr' or 'sg') with no internal structure. By introducing complexes of type *noun, verb*, etc. as values of HEAD, we have introduced complex values for features: feature structures within feature structures. This is a technique that will serve us well in the chapters to come. Moreover, it will be of immediate use in providing us with a simple way to express the relation between a headed phrase and its head daughter. That is, the Head Feature Principle (given below) can be stated simply in terms of the unification of HEAD specifications.

In a similar vein, we can now improve our treatment of agreement by introducing a new feature called AGR, whose value will be a feature structure containing the features NUM and PER. That is, AGR contains

---

[9]This analysis will in fact be revised in the next chapter, where these features are used only for nouns and determiners.

[10]We might instead introduce some mechanism for directly stipulating dependencies between values of different features – such as a statement that the existence of a value for AUX implies that the value for POS is 'verb'. (For a theory that incorporates just such a mechanism, see Gazdar et al. (1985).) But such a mechanism is unnecessary, given the availability of types in our theory.

just the information that matters for agreement.[11] Since we need to have agreement features specified on phrases as well as on their heads, AGR must be a head feature. Hence, it shows up in feature structures like (23).

(23)
$$\left[\text{HEAD} \quad \begin{bmatrix} noun \\ \text{AGR} \quad \begin{bmatrix} \text{PER} & \text{3rd} \\ \text{NUM} & \text{pl} \end{bmatrix} \end{bmatrix} \right]$$

Now we have a more compact way to say that two elements agree with respect to all agreement features: we say that their AGR specifications are unified.

The type hierarchy for the parts of speech introduced in this section is summarized in (24), which also indicates the features declared to be appropriate for each individual type.

(24)

So far, we have done two things: (i) we have identified the head daughter in a headed rule and (ii) we have bundled together (within the HEAD value) all the feature specifications that the head daughter must share with its mother. With these two adjustments in place, we are now in a position to simplify the grammar of headed phrases.

First we simplify all the headed rules: they no longer mention anything about number or the part of speech – the information specified within the HEAD value.

(25) a.
$$\begin{bmatrix} phrase \end{bmatrix} \to \text{H} \begin{bmatrix} word \\ \text{VAL} & \text{itr} \end{bmatrix}$$

b.
$$\begin{bmatrix} phrase \end{bmatrix} \to \text{H} \begin{bmatrix} word \\ \text{VAL} & \text{tr} \end{bmatrix} \text{NP}$$

c.
$$\begin{bmatrix} phrase \end{bmatrix} \to \text{H} \begin{bmatrix} word \\ \text{VAL} & \text{dtr} \end{bmatrix} \text{NP} \quad \text{NP}$$

Recall that the element labeled 'H' in the above rules is the head daughter.

---

[11]Formally, this will be specified by defining a type *agreement-category* and saying that the features NUM and PER are appropriate only for entities of this type.

Second, we state the Head Feature Principle as a general constraint governing all trees built by headed rules.

(26) Head Feature Principle (HFP)

In any headed phrase, the HEAD value of the mother and the HEAD value of the head daughter must be unified.

The HFP makes our rules simpler by factoring out those properties common to all headed phrases, and making them conditions that will quite generally be part of the trees defined by our grammar. By formulating the HFP in terms of unification of HEAD values, we allow information specified by the rule, information present on the daughter or the mother, or information required by some other constraint all to be amalgamated, as long as that information is compatible.

3.5 Trees and Phrase Structure

3.5.1 The Formal System: an informal account

At this point, we must address the general question of how rules, lexical entries and principles like the HFP interact to define linguistic structures. Our earlier discussion of the question in Chapter 2 requires some revision, now that we have introduced feature structures and types. In the case of simple context-free grammars, descriptions and structures are in simple correspondence: in CFG, each local subtree (that is, a mother node with its daughters) corresponds in a straightforward fashion to a rule of the grammar. All of the information in that local subtree comes directly from the rule. There is no reason to draw a distinction between the linguistic objects and the grammar's descriptions of them. But now that rules, lexical entries and principles like the HFP all contribute partial information about linguistic tokens, we must take care to specify how these partial descriptions are amalgamated and how the grammar specifies which expressions are grammatical.

The distinction between descriptions and the structures they describe is fundamental. We use feature structures as our models of linguistic entities. Consider what this meant for the feature structures we used to model universities, departments and individuals. Each such model is assumed to have all the properties relevant to understanding the university system; this includes (for individuals) a name, a birthday, a telephone number (let's assume), and so forth. The objects we take as models are thus complete in relevant respects.[12] Contrast this with descriptions of

---

[12]Of course, a model and the thing it is a model of differ with respect to certain irrelevant properties. Our models of university individuals should omit any irrelevant properties that all such individuals presumably have, ranging from hair color to grandmothers' middle names to disposition with respect to Indian food.

university individuals. These come in various degrees of completeness. A description may be partial in not specifying values for every feature, in specifying only part of the (complex) value of a feature, in failing to specify a type, or in specifying nothing at all. A complete description of some entity will presumably be satisfied by only one thing – the entity in question. An empty description is satisfied by all the entities in the modeling domain. Any nonempty partial description is satisfied by some things in the modeling domain, and not by others.

Our theory of language works the same way. We use feature structures and trees to model expressions like words and phrases; we also use feature structures to model other things like grammatical categories. Since the structures we use are models, they too are complete (or RE-SOLVED) with respect to all linguistically relevant properties. So a given word (token), say a pronoun, is a feature structure that has a determinate value for number – it is either singular or plural. Likewise, it is determinately 1st, 2nd or 3rd person. The only kind of thing that could be indeterminate – underspecified for this kind of information – is a feature structure description.

Grammars are linguistic descriptions; resolved feature structures and tree structures are the kinds of things that these descriptions describe. The grammar is successful to the extent that it can be shown that these structures – its models – have properties that are in correspondence with our observations about how the language (out there in the world, in society, or in people's heads) really is.

As we start to get more precise about our grammar, it will be important not to confuse linguistic structures and their descriptions. With this goal in mind, let us introduce a notational distinction. We will continue to use square bracket matrices (or ATTRIBUTE VALUE MATRICES) for feature structure descriptions, and whenever we want to make reference to a resolved feature structure model, we will use box diagrams. Thus the lexical entry for the noun *fish* will include a category description like the one shown in (27).

(27)

$$\left\langle \text{fish} \,, \begin{bmatrix} word \\ \text{HEAD} & \begin{bmatrix} noun \\ \text{AGR} & \begin{bmatrix} \text{PER} & \text{3rd} \end{bmatrix} \end{bmatrix} \\ \text{VAL} & \text{itr} \end{bmatrix} \right\rangle$$

We will interpret this lexical entry as a word description that has two distinct word structure models, corresponding to the category of the singular word *fish* and that of the plural word *fish*. We will take these word structures, illustrated in (28), to be nonbranching trees whose mother is a resolved feature structure satisfying the description in (27).

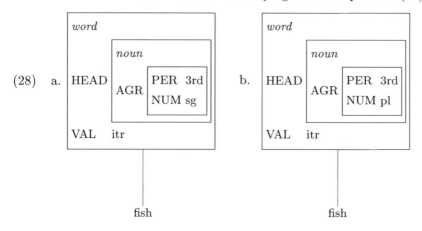

(28) a.

b.

fish

fish

As our grammar becomes more fully developed, there will in fact be more than two models for this description, each exhibiting a unique determination for such properties as mass vs. count, nominative vs. accusative case, and so forth. It is the goal of a grammar to enumerate all these linguistic entities (structures assumed to correspond to bits of reality) and to correctly describe their grammatical properties.

Phrase structures are not different in kind from word structures, except that they are licensed by grammar rules, rather than lexical entries. In our theory, a grammar rule is in fact viewed as a very general description of a certain kind of phrase, one that is satisfied by infinitely many resolved phrase structures. The purpose of principles like the Head Feature Principle then is to constrain the set of phrase structure models. So if we reconsider the grammar rule in (25a), repeated here as (29),

$$(29) \qquad \left[phrase\right] \rightarrow \quad H\left[\begin{matrix} word \\ VAL \quad itr \end{matrix}\right]$$

we see that there are four conceivable phrase structure models containing the word structures illustrated in (28), namely those in (30).

(30) Four Phrase Structures

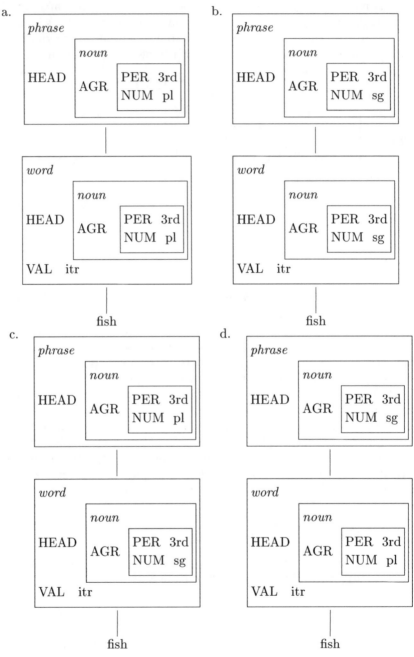

Without further principles, all of these resolved phrase structures would satisfy the rule in (29). By adding the HFP to our grammar, we rule out the phrase structures in (30c,d) as models of (29), because in each of these structures the HEAD value of the highest node fails to agree with that of its head daughter.

So the way our theory works is in terms of a notion of constraint satisfaction:

(31) A phrase structure is well-formed just in case each local subtree within it either:
1. satisfies a lexical entry, or
2. satisfies some grammar rule and all grammatical principles (e.g. the HFP).

This is quite similar to the way theories and models of them are presented in other sciences.[13]

As we develop our grammar to deal with more intricate phenomena, we will have occasion to introduce more grammatical features into our feature structures. For this reason, it would quickly become cumbersome to illustrate details of our analyses in terms of the resolved word and phrase structures that satisfy them. To avoid this problem, in the rest of this book we will present analyses in terms of descriptions of these structures, or STRUCTURAL DESCRIPTIONS (SDs), which are the amalgamation of constraints from lexical entries, grammar rules, and relevant grammatical principles. This will allow us to continue to use familiar, tree-like objects throughout our discussions, but without having to specify values for irrelevant features.

Descriptions of word structures will be called LEXICAL SDs and descriptions of phrase structures will be called PHRASAL SDs. A lexical SD is a tree diagram with two nodes: the lower node is a form that appears as the first member of a lexical entry, and the upper node is any word description that is an EXTENSION of the one that is the lexical entry's second member.[14] A well-formed description A is an extension of a description B (or alternatively 'B subsumes A') just in case A contains all the information in B, and possibly some more.

For phrases, the matter is slightly more complex. There are a number of constraints that we want to include in a well-formed phrasal SD. First of all, the mother and daughters of each local subtree of a phrasal SD must include all the information provided by the grammar rule that

---

[13]We will leave the intuitive notion of 'satisfaction' unexplicated for the moment, postponing a more formal presentation of our theory until Chapter 6.
[14]We ignore compound words throughout.

licensed that subtree. In addition, these local subtrees need to 'unify in' the information that comes from constraints like the HFP.

3.5.2 An Example

Consider the sentence *Fish swim*. Let's suppose that the lexical entry for *fish* is underspecified for number, as shown above (repeated in (32)), and that the lexical entry for the plural form *swim* is underspecified for person as shown in (32b):

(32) a.

$$\left\langle \text{fish} , \begin{bmatrix} word \\ \text{HEAD} & \begin{bmatrix} noun \\ \text{AGR} & \begin{bmatrix} \text{PER} & \text{3rd} \end{bmatrix} \end{bmatrix} \\ \text{VAL} & \text{itr} \end{bmatrix} \right\rangle$$

b.

$$\left\langle \text{swim} , \begin{bmatrix} word \\ \text{HEAD} & \begin{bmatrix} verb \\ \text{AGR} & \begin{bmatrix} \text{NUM} & \text{pl} \end{bmatrix} \end{bmatrix} \\ \text{VAL} & \text{itr} \end{bmatrix} \right\rangle$$

Given these two lexical entries, the following are both lexical SDs, according to our theory:

(33) a.

$$\begin{bmatrix} word \\ \text{HEAD} & \begin{bmatrix} noun \\ \text{AGR} & \begin{bmatrix} \text{PER} & \text{3rd} \end{bmatrix} \end{bmatrix} \\ \text{VAL} & \text{itr} \end{bmatrix}$$

|

fish

b.

$$\begin{bmatrix} word \\ \text{HEAD} & \begin{bmatrix} verb \\ \text{AGR} & \begin{bmatrix} \text{NUM} & \text{pl} \end{bmatrix} \end{bmatrix} \\ \text{VAL} & \text{itr} \end{bmatrix}$$

|

swim

Note that the lexical SDs in (33) are MINIMAL, that is, they specify exactly the same information that we find in the lexical entries (32a,b).

These SDs can now be embedded within larger SDs sanctioned by the rule in (29), as illustrated in (34a,b).

(34) a.

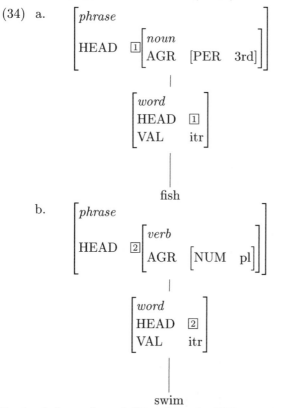

b.

Both of these phrasal SDs obey the HFP, as the values of HEAD (and hence the values for all features within HEAD, e.g. AGR) on the mother are identified with those on the head daughter. Note further that the AGR values of (34a) and (34b) are distinct, but compatible.

And finally, assuming we enforce agreement as before, by constraining our S rule as shown in (35), then we will build sentence descriptions like the one shown in (36). The symbol 'S' here is of course just an abbreviation for a feature structure description of a sort yet to be determined.

It is at this level that the real effect of unification is seen. The AGR values of the two daughters of S in (36) are unified, as they must be because the values for these features are unified in the rule (35) and our

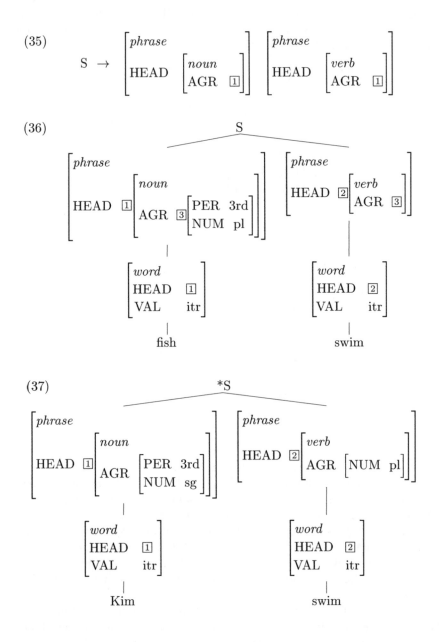

theory therefore requires that these values be identified in any tree constructed in accordance with that rule. The unified AGR value contains the two different pieces of compatible information, one coming from each of the phrase's daughters. Note that the lexical SDs contained in this phrasal SD are not minimal. Because the AGR values are identified at the highest level of structure in (36), the AGR information in each lexical subtree includes the information from both the noun *fish* and the verb *swim*.

Crucially, given our theory, the rule in (35) cannot give rise to an SD like (37), where the NP and VP daughters contain conflicting AGR information. In this way, the various constructs of our theory work together to rule out certain sentences as inconsistent with the simultaneous satisfaction of all relevant constraints. The only resolved feature structure that can be built from the lexical entries and grammar rules we have been discussing is the following one, of which (36) is a minimal description:

(38)

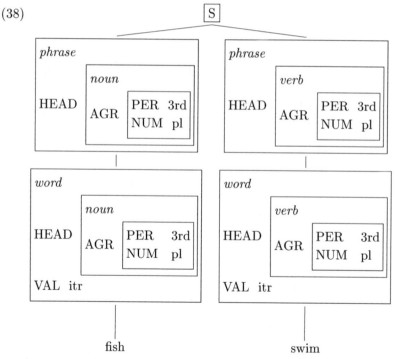

In short, the theory we have begun to sketch provides a precise MODEL-THEORETIC account of which expressions of a language are grammatical, which potential expressions are ungrammatical, which expressions are ambiguous, and so forth. The account proceeds by expressing generalizations in terms of a CFG-like conception of grammar rules, underspecified descriptions, and general constraints like the Head Feature Principle.

Somewhere along the line, of course, an adequate grammar will need to specify the well-formed 'stand alone' utterances of the language: the phrases that can be used in isolation to express a complete message are those whose mother is of the category S.[15] But we are not quite ready yet to define the notion 'S'. This will emerge clearly only after we consider the feature structures of phrases a bit more carefully, as we do in the next chapter.

⚠ Problem 2: Applying the Rules

The grammar just illustrated in the text, which we may refer to as $\mathbf{G}_2$ may be summarized as follows:

Rules of $\mathbf{G}_2$:

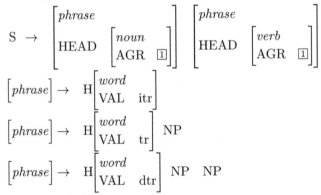

$$
\begin{bmatrix} phrase \end{bmatrix} \rightarrow \ \text{H} \begin{bmatrix} word \\ \text{VAL} \quad \text{itr} \end{bmatrix}
$$

$$
\begin{bmatrix} phrase \end{bmatrix} \rightarrow \ \text{H} \begin{bmatrix} word \\ \text{VAL} \quad \text{tr} \end{bmatrix} \ \text{NP}
$$

$$
\begin{bmatrix} phrase \end{bmatrix} \rightarrow \ \text{H} \begin{bmatrix} word \\ \text{VAL} \quad \text{dtr} \end{bmatrix} \ \text{NP} \quad \text{NP}
$$

Sample Lexicon of $\mathbf{G}_2$:

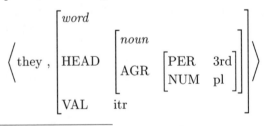

---

[15]This matter is actually more complex than it might seem, given that single word exclamations (e.g. *Help!*) can also express complete messages in isolation.

$$\left\langle \text{sing} \ , \ \begin{bmatrix} \textit{word} \\ \text{HEAD} & \begin{bmatrix} \textit{verb} \\ \text{AGR} & \begin{bmatrix} \text{NUM} & \text{pl} \end{bmatrix} \end{bmatrix} \\ \text{VAL} & \text{itr} \end{bmatrix} \right\rangle$$

A. Formulate a lexical entry for the word *sings* and explain how this entry interacts with other aspects of $\mathbf{G}_2$ so as to rule out unacceptable examples like *They sings*.

B. Formulate a feature structure version of the following rule (note that the head daughter is a word):   NP → (D) N
   Make sure that your rule is compatible with $\mathbf{G}_2$ and that it specifies all identities of feature values required to answer the remaining parts of this problem.

C. Give precise lexical entries for the determiners ([HEAD *det*]) *a* and *many*.

D. Demonstrate precisely how your answers to (B) and (C) work together to account for the following data:
   (i) *a birds
   (ii) *many bird

E. Explain (by constructing lexical entries and illustrating which rules cannot be applied) precisely how your analysis of NPs interacts with the rule for expanding S to explain the following examples.
   (iii) *The bird sing.
   (iv) *Many birds sings.

3.6   Conclusion

The introduction of features has given us a formal mechanism for talking about ways in which sets of words (and phrases) behave both alike and differently. By allowing embedded feature structures, underspecifying categories, and formulating general constraints stating identities that must hold in well-formed trees, we have been able to generalize our phrase structure rules and reduce their number. This in turn has led us to carefully distinguish between our grammar rules, the resolved structures that satisfy them, and the (partial) descriptions of those structures that we use throughout.

   The theory we are developing is still closely related to standard CFG, yet it is somewhat more abstract. We no longer think of our phrase structure rules as specifying all the information that labels the nodes of trees.

Rather, the rules, the lexicon, and some general principles – of which the HFP is the first example – all place certain constraints on trees, and any imaginable tree is well formed so long as it conforms to these constraints. In this way, our grammar continues to be constraint-based, with the rules, lexical entries, and general principles all contributing to linguistic descriptions and hence placing partial constraints on the well-formed structures of the language.

But the changes introduced in this chapter are not yet sufficient. They still leave us with three rules that have too much in common and could be collapsed. Moreover, as we will see in the next chapter, we have simplified the facts of agreement too much. And, as we mentioned above, our new feature-based system of rules doesn't allow us to reconstruct the category NOM. These problems will be dealt with in the next chapter, where we enrich our conception of features and of the lexicon, to allow still further simplification of the phrase structure rules.

3.7 Further Reading

One of the earliest (but often ignored) demonstrations of the descriptive power of feature structures is Harman (1963). Chomsky (1965) provides one of the earliest explicit discussions of syntactic features in generative grammar. The modern tradition of using complex feature structures (that is, features with feature structures as their values) begins with Kay (1979), Bear (1981), Bresnan (1982a), and Gazdar (1981) (see also Kaplan (1975) and Gazdar et al. (1985)). For an elementary discussion of the formal properties of unification and its use in grammatical description, see Shieber (1986). For differing and more detailed technical presentations of the logic of typed feature structures, see King (1989) and Carpenter (1992). The mathematics of tree structures is discussed by Partee et al. (1990).

4

Complex Feature Values

4.1 Introduction

By analyzing grammatical categories into features, we were able to generalize some of our phrase structure rules and eliminate others. This is not only a more compact way to represent syntactic information, it is also a way to encode systematically the fact that phrases of different types exhibit parallel structures. In addition, the analysis predicts that different phrase types generally will be similarly structured. In particular, the rules we gave in the previous chapter suggest that lexical head daughters in English uniformly occur at the left edge of their phrases.[1]

Of course, VPs and PPs are consistently head-initial, but it's not completely clear that NPs exhibit the same head-first pattern. For example, NPs may take determiners and adjectives before the lexical head, as in *the noisy dogs*. Recall that in our earlier treatment, NPs had an intermediate level of structure – every NP contained a NOM consituent; and every NOM contained a lexical head – a noun. This mode of analysis allowed us to maintain the generalization that the lexical head daughter is always the leftmost element under its mother node. It seems desirable, then, to find a way of reconstructing the NOM analysis within our new, feature-based theory.

Another motivation for revising our current analysis is that our rules are still not maximally general. We have three distinct rules introducing lexical heads, one for each of the three valences. We would like to consolidate these. Moreover, these three valences are far from the only possible environments lexical heads may require. Consider the examples in (1).

---

[1]This is not true in some other languages, e.g. in Japanese, the lexical head daughters are phrase-final, resulting in SOV (Subject-Object-Verb) ordering, as well as noun-final NPs.

(1) a. Pat relies on Kim.
     b. *Pat relies.
     c. The child put the toy on the table.
     d. *The child put the toy.
     e. The teacher became angry with the students.
     f. *The teacher became.
     g. The jury believed the witness lied.

Examples (1a,b) show that some verbs require following PPs; (1c,d) show that some verbs must be followed by both an NP and a PP; (1e,f) show a verb that can be followed by a kind of phrase we have not yet discussed, called an adjective phrase (AP); and (1g) shows a verb that can be followed by an S. We say only that *became* CAN be followed by an AP and that *believed* CAN be followed by an S, because they can also appear in sentences like *Pat became an astronaut* and *Pat believed the story*, in which they are followed by NPs. In fact, it is extremely common for verbs to be able to appear in multiple environments. Similarly, (2) shows that *ate*, like many other English verbs, can be used either transitively or intransitively.

(2) The guests ate (the cheese).

Facts like these show that the number of values of VAL must be far greater than three. This in itself would not be problematic, except that our current formalism, as developed in the previous chapter, requires a separate phrase structure rule for each value of VAL. This is an unwanted redundancy, for the lexical distinctions would be encoded twice: once in the phrase structure rules and once in the (many) new values of VAL that would be required.

4.2   Complements

Intuitively, we would like to have our rule simply say that a phrase (a VP, in the cases above) may consist of a lexical head (a V, in these cases) followed by whatever other phrases the lexical head requires. We could then relegate to the lexicon the task of specifying for each word what elements must appear together with (or co-occur with) that word. In this section, we develop a way to do just this. It involves enriching our conception of valence features in a way somewhat analogous to what we did with grammatical categories in the previous chapter.

Before we begin the discussion of this analysis, however, let us consider briefly the status of the kinds of co-occurrence restrictions we have been talking about. For this discussion (and much else that follows), it will be convenient to have a term for the elements that characteristically co-occur with a lexical head – that is, for things like the phrases that occur after the verbs in (1). The term COMPLEMENT (of the head) is more or less standard and will be used throughout this text.

It has sometimes been argued that the number and type of complements a verb takes is fully determined by its meaning. For example, the verb *disappear* is used to describe events involving a single entity (expressed by its subject); *deny*'s semantics involves events with two participants, one typically human and the other a proposition; and an event described by *hand* must include three participants: the person who does the handing, the thing handed, and the recipient of the transaction. Correspondingly, *disappear* takes no complements, only a subject; *deny* takes a subject and a complement, which may be either an NP (as in *The defendant denied the charges*) or an S (as in *The defendant denied he was guilty*); and *hand* takes a subject and two NP complements (or one NP and one PP complement).

It is undeniable that the semantics of a verb is intimately related to its valence. There is, however, a certain amount of syntactic arbitrariness to it, as well. For example, the words *eat, dine*, and *devour* all denote activities necessarily involving both a consumer of food and the food itself. Hence, if a word's valence were fully determined by its meanings, one might expect that all three would be simple transitives, requiring a subject and an NP complement (that is, a direct object). But this expectation would be wrong: *dine* is intransitive, *devour* is obligatorily transitive, and (as noted above), *eat* can be used intransitively or transitively.

(3) a. The guests devoured the meal.
    b. *The guests devoured.
    c. *The guests dined the meal.
    d. The guests dined.
    e. The guests ate the meal.
    f. The guests ate.

Thus, though we recognize that there is an important link between meaning and valence, we will continue to specify valence syntactically. We will say more about the connection between meaning and valence – and more generally about the syntax-semantics interface – in later chapters.

4.3 The COMPS Feature

In our current grammar, the lexical entry for a verb like *deny* would specify that it is [VAL tr]. This ensures that it can only appear in word structures that are specified as [VAL tr], and such word structures can be used to build larger structures only by using the rule of our grammar that introduces an immediately following NP. Hence, *deny* has to be followed by an NP.[2]

In effect, the value of the VAL feature in this system functions as a pointer to the relevant phrase structure rule for licensing the verb in question. In fact, the values of VAL correspond one-to-one with the phrase structure rules that assign the appropriate kinds of complements to the lexical head daughters. This redundancy is another we would like to eliminate from our grammar.

An alternative approach to complement selection is to use features directly in licensing complements – that is, to have a feature whose value specifies what the complements must be. We will now make this intuitive idea explicit. First, recall that in the last chapter we allowed some features (e.g. HEAD, AGR) to take values that are feature structures themselves. If we replace VAL with such a feature, we can allow its value to state directly what the word's complement must be. So we propose to replace VAL with a feature-valued feature, which we call COMPLEMENTS (COMPS). The value of COMPS for *deny* can simply be NP – the feature structure description in (4):

(4) $\begin{bmatrix} phrase \\ \text{HEAD} \quad noun \end{bmatrix}$

Similarly, we can indicate that a verb takes another type of complement: *rely, become,* and *believe,* for example, can take COMPS values of PP, AP, and S, respectively.[3] Optional complements, such as the object of *eat* can be indicated using parentheses; that is, the lexical entry for *eat* can specify [COMPS (NP)]. Likewise, we can indicate alternative choices for complements using the vertical bar notation introduced in the discussion of regular expressions in Chapter 2. So the entry for *deny* or *believe* includes the specification: [COMPS NP | S].

Of course there is a problem with this proposal: it does not cover verbs like *hand* and *put* that require more than one complement. But it's not hard to invent a straightforward way of modifying the COMPS analysis to let it encompass multiple complements. Instead of treating the value of COMPS as a single feature structure, we will let it be a LIST of feature structures. Intuitively, the list specifies a sequence of

---

[2]As noted earlier, we have not dealt with the other possible environment for *deny*, namely the one where it is followed by a clause. We ignore this problem for the moment, but the analysis developed in this chapter provides a way of dealing with it.

[3]We have not yet said anything about how S is analyzed in terms of feature structures. Later in this chapter, however, we will present a treatment of S as an abbreviation for a feature structure, just like other category names.

categories corresponding to the complements that the word combines with. So, for example, the COMPS values for *deny, become,* and *eat* will be lists of length one. For *hand,* the COMPS value will be a list of length two, namely ⟨NP, NP⟩.[4] For verbs taking no complements, like *disappear*, the value of COMPS will be ⟨ ⟩ (a list of length zero). We interpret this to mean that trees containing the verb in question will be well formed only if the sisters of the V-node are compatible with the categories specified on the list. For example, *rely* will only be allowed in trees where the VP dominates a V and a PP.

Now we can collapse all the different rules for expanding a phrase into a lexical head (H) and other material. We can just say:

(5) Head-Complement Rule

$$\begin{bmatrix} phrase \\ \text{COMPS} \quad \langle \rangle \end{bmatrix} \rightarrow \text{H} \begin{bmatrix} word \\ \text{COMPS} \quad \langle \boxed{1},...,\boxed{n} \rangle \end{bmatrix} \boxed{1} ... \boxed{n}$$

Thus, if a word is specified lexically as [COMPS ⟨AP⟩], it must co-occur with exactly one AP complement; if it is [COMPS ⟨NP, NP⟩], it must co-occur with exactly two NP complements, and so forth. Note that we also want (5) to allow for a phrase that contains a head daughter but no complements (letting $n = 0$). So if the head daughter is lexically specified as [COMPS ⟨ ⟩], it must appear as the only daughter in a phrase structure licensed by (5). Finally, the mother of any structure licensed by (5), which we will term a HEAD-COMPLEMENT PHRASE, must be specified as [COMPS ⟨ ⟩], because that mother must satisfy the description on the left-hand side of the rule.[5]

In short, the COMPS list of a lexical entry specifies a word's co-occurrence requirements; and the COMPS list of a phrasal node is empty. So, in particular, a V must have sisters that match all the feature structures in its COMPS value, and the VP that it heads has the empty list as its COMPS value and hence cannot combine with complements. The Head-Complement Rule, as stated, requires all complements to be realized as sisters to the lexical head.[6]

If you think in terms of building the tree bottom-up, starting with

---

[4]We use angle brackets to designate lists.

[5]Note that by underspecifying the complements introduced by this rule – not even requiring them to be phrases, for example – we are implicitly leaving open the possibility that some complements will be nonphrasal. This will become important in the analysis of negation presented in Chapter 13.

[6]This appears well motivated for English, but our general theory allows us to write a Head-Complement Rule for some other language that allows some of the complements to be introduced higher in the tree structure. For example, structures like the one in (i) would be allowed by a version of the Head-Complement Rule that required

the verb as head, then the verb has certain demands that have to be satisfied before a complete, or 'saturated', constituent is formed. On this conception, the complements can be thought of as being 'cancelled off' of the head daughter's COMPS list in the process of building a headed phrase. We illustrate this with the VP *put flowers in a vase*: the verb *put* requires both a direct object NP and a PP complement, so its COMPS value is ⟨NP, PP⟩. The requisite NP and PP will both be sisters to the V, as in (6), as all three combine to form a VP, i.e. a verbal phrase whose complement requirements have been fulfilled.

(6)

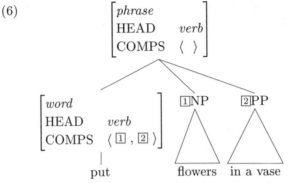

As is evident from this example, we assume that the elements in the

---

neither that the head daughter be of type *word* nor that the mother have an empty COMPS list:

(i)

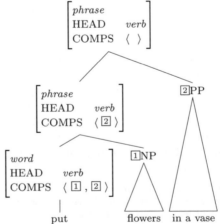

Such grammatical variations might be regarded as 'parameters' that are set differently in particular languages. That is, it may be that all languages manifest the Head-Complement Rule, but there are minor differences in the way languages incorporate the rule into their grammar. The order of the head and the complements is another such parameter of variation.

value of COMPS occur in the same order as they appear in the sentence. We will continue to make this assumption, though ultimately a more sophisticated treatment of linear ordering of phrases in sentences may be necessary.

A common source of confusion is that some kinds of constituents, notably PPs, can function either as complements or as modifiers. This often raises the question of how to analyze a particular PP: should it be treated as a complement, licensed by a PP on the COMPS list of a nearby word, or should it be analyzed as a modifier, introduced by a different grammar rule? Some cases are clear. For example, we know that a PP is a complement when the choice of preposition is idiosyncratically restricted by another word, such as the verb *rely*, which requires a PP headed by *on* or *upon*. In fact, PPs that are obligatorily required by a head (e.g. the directional PP required by *put*) can fairly safely be treated as complements. Conversely, there are certain kinds of PPs that seem to be able to co-occur with almost any kind of verb, such as temporal or locative PPs, and these are almost always analyzed as modifiers. PPs of a kind that can iterate, as in examples like *We celebrated in the streets in the rain on Tuesday in the morning*, are generally treated as modifiers. The underlying intuition here is that complements refer to the essential participants in the situation denoted, whereas modifiers serve to further refine the description of the situation. This is not a precisely defined distinction, and there are problems with trying to make it into a formal criterion. Consequently, there are difficult borderline cases that syntacticians disagree about. Nevertheless, there is considerable agreement that the distinction between complements and modifiers is a real one that should be reflected in a formal theory of grammar.

Returning to our analysis of complements, notice that although we have motivated our treatment of complements entirely in terms of verbs and verb phrases, we have formulated our analysis to be more general. In particular, our grammar of head-complement structures allows adjectives, nouns, and prepositions to take complements of various types. The following examples suggest that, like verbs, these kinds of words exhibit a range of valence possibilities.

(7) Adjectives
    a. The children are happy (with the ice cream).
    b. The children are fond of ice cream.
    c.*The children are fond.
    d. The children are happy (that they have ice cream).
    e.*The children are fond that they have ice cream.

(8) Nouns

    a. A magazine (about crime) appeared on the newsstands.

    b.*Newsweek about crime appeared on the newsstands.

    c. Newsweek appeared on the newsstands.

    d. The report (that crime was declining) surprised many people.

    e.*The book that crime was declining surprised many people.

    f. The book surprised many people.

(9) Prepositions

    a. The storm arrived after the picnic.

    b. The storm arrived after we ate lunch.

    c. The storm arrived during the picnic.

    d.*The storm arrived during we ate lunch.

    e.*The storm arrived while the picnic.

    f. The storm arrived while we ate lunch.

⚠ **Problem 1: Valence Variations**

In this problem, you may use NP, VP, etc. as abbreviations for the feature structures on COMPS lists.

    A. What does the grammaticality of sentences like *Kim put the book here/there* suggest about the COMPS and HEAD values of the words *here* and *there*?

    B. What is the COMPS value for the adjective *fond*?

    C. Assume that motion verbs like *jump, move*, etc. take an optional PP complement. Given that, what do the following examples tell you about the COMPS values of the lexical entries of the prepositions *out, from* and *of*:

      (i) Kim jumped out of the bushes.

      (ii) Bo jumped out from the bushes.

      (iii) Lee moved from under the bushes.

      (iv) Leslie jumped out from under the bushes.

      (v) Dana jumped from the bushes.

      (vi) Chris ran out the door.

      (vii)*Kim jumped out of from the bushes.

      (viii) Kim jumped out.

      (ix)*Kim jumped from.

    D. Based on the following data, sketch the lexical entries for the words *grew* (in the 'become' sense, not the 'cultivate' sense), *seemed, happy*, and *close*.

      (i) They seemed happy (to me).

(ii) Lee seemed an excellent choice (to me).
(iii) They grew happy.
(iv)*They grew a monster (to me).
(v)*They grew happy to me.
(vi) They grew close to me.
(vii) They seemed close to me to Sandy.

[*Note: APs have an internal structure analogous to that of VPs. Though no adjectives select NP complements (in English), there are some adjectives that select PP complements (e.g. to me), and some that do not.*]

4.4 Specifiers

Co-occurrence restrictions are not limited to complements. As we have noted in earlier chapters, certain verb forms appear with only certain types of subjects. In particular, in the present tense, English subjects and verbs must agree in number. Likewise, certain determiners co-occur only with nouns of a particular number.

(10) a. This dog barked.
b. *This dogs barked.
c. *These dog barked.
d. These dogs barked.

Moreover, some determiners are restricted to occur only with 'mass' nouns (e.g. *furniture, footwear, information*), and others only with 'count' nouns (e.g. *chair, shoe, fact*):

(11) a. Much furniture was broken.
b. *A furniture was broken.
c. *Much chair was broken.
d. A chair was broken.

We can handle such co-occurrence restrictions in much the same way that we dealt with the requirements that heads impose on their complements. First, we introduce the term SPECIFIER to refer to both subjects and determiners. We then introduce the feature SPECIFIER (SPR), with which we can state the co-occurrence restrictions for heads and the specifiers they select. On analogy with COMPS, we make the value of SPR a list. This decision may strike some readers as odd, since sentences only have a single subject and NPs never have more than one determiner. But making SPR list-valued provides a uniform way of formulating the idea that a particular valence requirement is unfulfilled (the valence feature – that is, COMPS or SPR – has a nonempty value) or else is fulfilled (the value of the valence feature is the empty list).

We can now define the category NOM in terms of the following feature structure descriptions:

(12)
$$\text{NOM} = \begin{bmatrix} phrase \\ \text{HEAD} & noun \\ \text{COMPS} & \langle \ \rangle \\ \text{SPR} & \langle \begin{bmatrix} \text{HEAD} & det \end{bmatrix} \rangle \end{bmatrix}$$

Notice the similarity between (12) and (what is now) the feature specification for VP:

(13)
$$\text{VP} = \begin{bmatrix} phrase \\ \text{HEAD} & verb \\ \text{COMPS} & \langle \ \rangle \\ \text{SPR} & \langle \text{NP} \rangle \end{bmatrix}$$

Both (12) and (13) are of type *phrase* with empty COMPS lists and a single element in their SPR lists. Both are intermediate between lexical categories (type *word*, with possibly nonempty COMPS lists) and SAT-URATED phrases – that is, phrases with both their COMPS and SPR lists empty.

Similarly, we can now introduce a verbal category that is analogous in all relevant respects to the saturated category NP. It is just the feature structure analogue of the familiar category S.

(14)
$$\text{NP} = \begin{bmatrix} phrase \\ \text{HEAD} & noun \\ \text{COMPS} & \langle \ \rangle \\ \text{SPR} & \langle \ \rangle \end{bmatrix} \qquad \text{S} = \begin{bmatrix} phrase \\ \text{HEAD} & verb \\ \text{COMPS} & \langle \ \rangle \\ \text{SPR} & \langle \ \rangle \end{bmatrix}$$

Because NP and S now have a parallel formulation in terms of feature structures and parallel constituent structures, we may collapse our old rules for expanding these categories (given in (15)) into a single rule, shown in (16), that sanctions all HEAD-SPECIFIER PHRASES.

(15) a. S → NP VP
     b. NP → (D) NOM

(16)   Head-Specifier Rule

$$\begin{bmatrix} phrase \\ \text{COMPS} & \langle \ \rangle \\ \text{SPR} & \langle \ \rangle \end{bmatrix} \rightarrow \boxed{2} \quad \text{H}\begin{bmatrix} phrase \\ \text{SPR} & \langle \boxed{2} \rangle \end{bmatrix}$$

Having consolidated the rules in this way, we need to explain more precisely how our treatment of the SPR feature can account for the various co-occurrence restrictions between heads and specifiers. These include the fact that the specifier daughter of a sentence (i.e. its subject) is an NP, whereas the specifier daughter of an NP is a D. They also include facts like those in (10)–(11), and the agreement between subjects and verbs, which will be dealt with in sections 4.6 and 4.7 below.

The first of these is relatively simple: the value for SPR in the lexical entries for nouns is the list ⟨ D ⟩, and in the lexical entries for verbs, it is the list ⟨ NP ⟩. Notice that this analysis entails that the lexical head's value for the SPR feature must be available at the nonlexical level where the specifier phrase is attached. Thus for the new rule in (16) to work, we will have to modify our Head-Complement Rule so that it 'passes' the SPR value of the lexical head 'up' to its mother.[7] We might thus add a stipulation to this effect, as shown in (17):

(17) Head-Complement Rule

$$
\begin{bmatrix} phrase \\ \text{SPR} \quad \boxed{a} \\ \text{COMPS} \quad \langle\,\rangle \end{bmatrix} \rightarrow \text{H} \begin{bmatrix} word \\ \text{SPR} \quad \boxed{a} \\ \text{COMPS} \quad \langle \boxed{1},...,\boxed{n} \rangle \end{bmatrix} \boxed{1} ... \boxed{n}
$$

(Note that here we are using the tag $\boxed{a}$ to designate neither an atomic value nor a feature structure, but rather a list of feature structures.[8])

The modification in (17) solves the problem of getting the SPR selection information from the lexical head up to VP or NOM – the phrase that will combine directly with the specifier (via our new rule (16)), but it does so at the cost of adding a stipulation to our rules. Moreover, more stipulations are needed if we consider additional rules. In particular, recall the rule for introducing PP modifiers, discussed in the previous chapter. Because no complements or specifiers are added by this rule, we do not want any cancellation from either of the head daughter's valence features. Hence, we would need to complicate the rule so as to transmit values for both valence features up from the head daughter to the mother, as shown in (18):

---

[7] At first glance, one might be tempted to accomplish this by making SPR a head feature, but in that case the statement of the HFP would have to be complicated, to allow rule (16) to introduce a discrepancy between the HEAD value of a mother and its head daughter.

[8] We will henceforth adopt the convention of using numbers to tag feature structures and letters to tag lists of feature structures.

(18)
$$\begin{bmatrix} phrase \\ \text{SPR} & \boxed{a} \\ \text{COMPS} & \boxed{b} \end{bmatrix} \rightarrow \text{H} \begin{bmatrix} phrase \\ \text{SPR} & \boxed{a} \\ \text{COMPS} & \boxed{b} \end{bmatrix} \text{PP}$$

Without some such constraint, our modifiers cannot combine with a VP head daughter to build another VP. It is time to contemplate a more general theory of how the valence features behave in headed phrases.

4.5   The Valence Principle

The intuitive idea in the previous section is quite straightforward: certain lexical entries specify what they can co-occur with by listing (as the value of the features COMPS and SPR) the particular kinds of dependents they select. And we formulated general rules, stating that all the head's COMPS members are 'discharged' in a head-complement phrase, and the item in the SPR value is discharged in a head-specifier phrase. But to make these rules work, we had to add constraints preserving valence specifications in all other instances: the mother in the Head-Specifier Rule preserves the head's COMPS value (the empty list); the mother in the Head-Complement Rule preserves the head's SPR value, and the mother in the Head-Modifier Rule must preserve both the COMPS value and the SPR value of the head. The operant generalization that can be factored out of our rules can be expressed as the following principle which, like the HFP, constrains the set of phrase structure models that satisfy our grammar rules:

(19) The Valence Principle
      Unless the rule says otherwise, the mother's SPR and COMPS values are identical to those of the head daughter.

By 'unless the rule says otherwise', we mean simply that the Valence Principle is enforced unless a particular grammar rule specifies both the mother's and the head daughter's value for some valence feature.

The effect of the Valence Principle is that (1) the appropriate elements mentioned in particular rules are canceled from the relevant valence specifications of the head daughter in head-complement or head-specifier phrases, and (2) all other valence specifications are simply passed up from head daughter to mother. Once we factor these constraints out of our headed rules and put them into a single principle, it again becomes possible to simplify our grammar rules. This is illustrated in (20).

(20) a. Head-Specifier Rule

$$\begin{bmatrix} phrase \\ \text{SPR} \quad \langle \, \rangle \end{bmatrix} \rightarrow \boxed{1} \quad H \begin{bmatrix} phrase \\ \text{SPR} \quad \langle \, \boxed{1} \, \rangle \end{bmatrix}$$

b. Head-Complement Rule

$$\begin{bmatrix} phrase \\ \text{COMPS} \quad \langle \, \rangle \end{bmatrix} \rightarrow H \begin{bmatrix} word \\ \text{COMPS} \quad \langle \boxed{1},...,\boxed{n} \rangle \end{bmatrix} \boxed{1} ... \boxed{n}$$

c. Head-Modifier Rule

$$\begin{bmatrix} phrase \end{bmatrix} \rightarrow H \begin{bmatrix} phrase \end{bmatrix} \text{PP}[...]$$

Our work is not yet done. We will modify the Head-Modifier Rule in the next chapter; in addition there are modifications of (20a,b) yet to be introduced. Nevertheless, the simplicity of the rules as formulated in (20) is striking.

Note that since head-specifier structures require a phrasal head and the Head-Complement Rule requires a lexical head, it follows that head-complement phrases must be embedded within head-specifier phrases (rather than vice versa), as shown in (21):

(21)

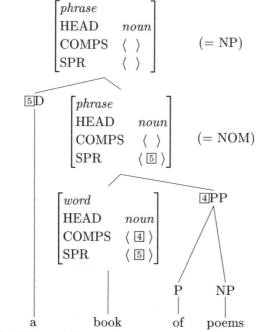

Thus COMPS cancellation happens at the NOM level and SPR cancellation happens at the NP level. The same is true of verbal structures:

complements must be introduced lower (within a VP) than specifiers (which appear as sisters to a VP head within S).

4.6 Subject-Verb Agreement Revisited

Let us now return to the problem of subject-verb agreement. Our earlier analysis assigned the feature AGR to both nouns and verbs, and one of our grammar rules stipulated that the AGR values of VPs and their subjects had to match. But our new analysis has no need to specify AGR values for VPs. Since VPs all select their subject via the SPR feature, what are traditionally referred to as 'plural verbs' can be treated simply in terms of the specification [SPR ⟨NP[AGR [NUM pl]]⟩]; 'singular verbs' can similarly be specified just as [SPR ⟨NP[AGR [NUM sg]]⟩]. Additional agreement features of verbs, VPs, or even S are simply unnecessary.

However, subject-verb agreement is a bit more complex than this, because it does not depend only on number. More specifically, English agreement also depends on PERSON. As noted earlier, we analyze person in terms of varying specifications for the feature PER. [PER 1st] is our notation for first person, that is, the pronouns *I* and *we*. [PER 2nd] denotes second person, which in English is always *you*. [PER 3rd] covers all nonpronominal NPs, as well as *he*, *she*, *it*, and *they*. Most present tense English verbs have one form when their subjects are third-person singular (namely a form ending in *-s*) and another form covering all other persons and numbers. The only verb whose present tense system makes finer distinctions than this is *be*, which has a special first-person singular form, *am* and an additional form *are* (appropriate wherever *am* and *is* are not).

We can couch our analysis of these verb forms in terms of a distinction between two kinds of values of the feature AGR. Suppose we call these two types *3sing* and *non-3sing*. The distinction among the third-person singular pronouns *he*, *she*, and *it* is attributed to a feature GEND(ER), with values *masc*, *fem*, and *neut*. GEND also differentiates among *him*, *her*, *it*, as well as among *himself*, *herself*, and *itself*. There is no motivation in English for assigning GEND to anything other than words that are third-person and singular.[9]

What this means is that we can set up our system so that the values of the feature AGR obey restrictions on the combinations of values of the

---

[9]This can be taken as independent evidence for the existence of *3sing* as a separate type – we can express this restriction by declaring the feature GEND as appropriate only for feature structures of the type *3sing*.

features PER and NUM. Instances of the type *3sing* obey the constraint shown in (22):

(22)
$$3sing \; : \; \begin{bmatrix} \text{PER} & \text{3rd} \\ \text{NUM} & \text{sg} \end{bmatrix}$$

And we enumerate the subtypes of *non-3sing* so as to include only first-person, second-person, or third-person plural specifications.[10] As a consequence of this analysis, the only possible values for the feature AGR (in English) are those described in (23).

(23)   Possible AGR Values

$$\begin{bmatrix} \textit{3sing} \\ \text{PER} & \text{3rd} \\ \text{NUM} & \text{sg} \\ \text{GEND} & \text{fem} \end{bmatrix} \quad \begin{bmatrix} \textit{3sing} \\ \text{PER} & \text{3rd} \\ \text{NUM} & \text{sg} \\ \text{GEND} & \text{masc} \end{bmatrix} \quad \begin{bmatrix} \textit{3sing} \\ \text{PER} & \text{3rd} \\ \text{NUM} & \text{sg} \\ \text{GEND} & \text{neut} \end{bmatrix}$$

$$\begin{bmatrix} \textit{non-3sing} \\ \text{PER} & \text{3rd} \\ \text{NUM} & \text{pl} \end{bmatrix} \quad \begin{bmatrix} \textit{non-3sing} \\ \text{PER} & \text{1st} \\ \text{NUM} & \text{sg} \end{bmatrix} \quad \begin{bmatrix} \textit{non-3sing} \\ \text{PER} & \text{1st} \\ \text{NUM} & \text{pl} \end{bmatrix}$$

$$\begin{bmatrix} \textit{non-3sing} \\ \text{PER} & \text{2nd} \\ \text{NUM} & \text{sg} \end{bmatrix} \quad \begin{bmatrix} \textit{non-3sing} \\ \text{PER} & \text{2nd} \\ \text{NUM} & \text{pl} \end{bmatrix}$$

A pronoun may specify one of these possibilities in its lexical entry; other elements, for example proper names, will have lexical entries whose AGR value is specified only as *3sing*, making these elements compatible in principle with any gender specification.

This treatment of the AGR values of nouns and NPs enables us to streamline our analysis of verbs. We can require that the lexical entries

---

[10]One organization of these subtypes is as in (i), with constraints defined as in (ii):

(i)   *non-3sing*

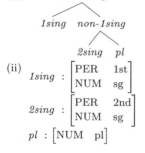

(ii)
$$1sing \; : \; \begin{bmatrix} \text{PER} & \text{1st} \\ \text{NUM} & \text{sg} \end{bmatrix}$$
$$2sing \; : \; \begin{bmatrix} \text{PER} & \text{2nd} \\ \text{NUM} & \text{sg} \end{bmatrix}$$
$$pl \; : \; \begin{bmatrix} \text{NUM} & \text{pl} \end{bmatrix}$$

for words like *walks*, *runs*, or *is* (all derived in later chapters by lexical rules) include the following specification:

$$(24) \quad \begin{bmatrix} \text{SPR} & \left\langle \begin{bmatrix} \text{HEAD} & \begin{bmatrix} noun \\ \text{AGR} & \textit{3sing} \end{bmatrix} \\ \text{COMPS} & \langle\,\rangle \\ \text{SPR} & \langle\,\rangle \end{bmatrix} \right\rangle \end{bmatrix}$$

The third-person singular proper noun *Kim* and the present-tense verb form *walks* thus have lexical entries like the following:

$$(25) \text{ a.} \quad \left\langle \text{Kim} \,, \begin{bmatrix} \text{HEAD} & \begin{bmatrix} noun \\ \text{AGR} & \textit{3sing} \end{bmatrix} \\ \text{COMPS} & \langle\,\rangle \\ \text{SPR} & \langle\,\rangle \end{bmatrix} \right\rangle$$

$$\text{b.} \quad \left\langle \text{walks} \,, \begin{bmatrix} \text{HEAD} & verb \\ \text{SPR} & \left\langle \begin{bmatrix} \text{HEAD} & \begin{bmatrix} noun \\ \text{AGR} & \textit{3sing} \end{bmatrix} \\ \text{COMPS} & \langle\,\rangle \\ \text{SPR} & \langle\,\rangle \end{bmatrix} \right\rangle \end{bmatrix} \right\rangle$$

Because AGR is a head feature, any NP that serves as the subject of a verb like *walks* will have to contain a lexical head noun (for example a proper noun like *Kim*) that is also specified as [AGR *3sing*]. This is a consequence of the HFP, which identifies the HEAD value of an NP with that of its head daughter. Thus verbs whose lexical entries include (24) will occur with NPs headed by third-person singular nouns, but never with plural nouns, or with first-person or second-person pronouns.

It is often assumed that it is necessary to posit separate lexical entries for present tense verb forms that take plural subjects and those that take singular, non-third person subjects, as sketched in (26a,b):

$$(26) \text{ a.} \quad \begin{bmatrix} \text{SPR} & \left\langle \begin{bmatrix} \text{HEAD} & \begin{bmatrix} noun \\ \text{AGR} & [\text{NUM} \quad \text{pl}] \end{bmatrix} \\ \text{COMPS} & \langle\,\rangle \\ \text{SPR} & \langle\,\rangle \end{bmatrix} \right\rangle \end{bmatrix}$$

b.

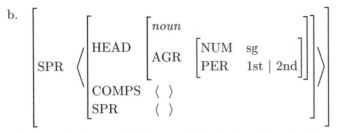

But such an analysis would fail to explain the fact that the former type of verb would always be identical in form to the latter: again, a suspicious loss of generalization in the lexicon.

Once we bifurcate the types of AGR values, as described above, this problem disappears. We need only a single kind of verb, one that includes the following lexical information:

$$(27) \quad \begin{bmatrix} \text{SPR} & \left\langle \begin{bmatrix} \text{HEAD} & \begin{bmatrix} noun \\ \text{AGR} & non\text{-}3sing \end{bmatrix} \\ \text{COMPS} & \langle \, \rangle \\ \text{SPR} & \langle \, \rangle \end{bmatrix} \right\rangle \end{bmatrix}$$

Verbs so specified project VPs that take subjects whose head nouns must bear *non-3sing* AGR values, and these, as described above, must either be first-person singular, second-person singular, or plural.[11]

Problem 2: The SPR Value of *am*
What would the SPR value in the lexical entry for *am* be?

4.7 Determiner-Noun Agreement

We have just seen how our new analysis of specifiers, taken together with the Head Feature Principle, provides an account of the fact that third-person singular verb forms (e.g. *walks*) take subject NPs headed by third-person singular nouns. But, as we saw in section 4.4, the specifiers of the phrases projected from these nouns also agree in number. In

---

[11]The disjunctions needed for describing classes of verbs are thus given by the type hierarchy, not by writing arbitrarily disjunctive lexical entries. One of the goals for a type-based grammar is to predict in this manner which disjunctions will be required for the grammatical analysis of a given language (or of language in general). A grammar that specifies a family of types consequently makes predictions about which classes of linguistic entities pattern together. A theory that simply specifies disjunctions wherever necessary makes no such predictions and is hence of considerably less explanatory value.

fact, the relevant data are slightly more complicated here, too. English
has determiners like *this* and *a*, which only appear with singular nouns,
plural determiners like *these* and *few*, which only appear with plural
nouns, and other determiners like *the*, which go either way. These facts
are illustrated in (28)–(30).

(28) a. This dog barked.
      b. *This dogs barked.
      c. A dog barked.
      d. *A dogs barked.

(29) a. *These dog barked.
      b. These dogs barked.
      c. *Few dog barked.
      d. Few dogs barked.

(30) a. The dog barked.
      b. The dogs barked.

In addition to the 'feature passing' that is guaranteed by the HFP,
there is systematic agreement of person and number between heads and
specifiers within the NP. To express this fact generally, we add the following constraint on all nouns:[12]

(31)   Nominal SPR Agreement (NSA):

Nouns must be specified as:
$$\begin{bmatrix} \text{HEAD} & \begin{bmatrix} \text{AGR} & \boxed{1} \end{bmatrix} \\ \text{SPR} & \left\langle \left(\begin{bmatrix} \text{AGR} & \boxed{1} \end{bmatrix} \right) \right\rangle \end{bmatrix}$$

The NSA requires that the AGR value of a noun be identified (unified) with that of its determiner, if the latter is realized. It thus makes
determiner-noun agreement a lexical fact about nouns. This account
presupposes that determiners and nouns both bear AGR specifications,
as illustrated in (32).

(32)

person, boat, a, this:
$$\begin{bmatrix} \text{AGR} & \begin{bmatrix} \text{PER} & \text{3rd} \\ \text{NUM} & \text{sg} \end{bmatrix} \end{bmatrix}$$

people, boats, few, these:
$$\begin{bmatrix} \text{AGR} & \begin{bmatrix} \text{PER} & \text{3rd} \\ \text{NUM} & \text{pl} \end{bmatrix} \end{bmatrix}$$

---

[12]Since we have not yet developed our account of word types, we do not yet have a
subtype of *word* that only words specified as [HEAD *noun*] belong to. In Chapter
8, the NSA will be stated as a constraint on the type *noun-lexeme*.

fish, the: $\begin{bmatrix} \text{AGR} & \begin{bmatrix} \text{PER} & \text{3rd} \end{bmatrix} \end{bmatrix}$

These lexical specifications, taken together with the NSA and the HFP, provide a complete account of the agreement data in (28) – (30) above.

In section 4.4 above, we also observed that some determiners are restricted to occur only with 'mass' nouns (e.g. *furniture*), and others only with 'count' nouns (e.g. *chair*):

(33) a.   Much furniture was broken.
      b. *A furniture was broken.
      c. *Much chair was broken.
      d.   A chair was broken.

The co-occurrence restriction illustrated in (33) – that is, the count noun/mass noun distinction – might, of course, be solely a semantic matter. The contrasting judgments in (33) are particularly striking, however, and may well warrant our treating the distinction as a matter of syntax. Assuming the syntactic account to be desirable (and such matters are often difficult to decide), we could analyze the data in (33) by introducing a feature COUNT. Certain determiners (e.g. *a* and *few*) will be lexically specified as [COUNT +] and others (e.g. *much*) will be lexically treated as [COUNT −]. Still others, such as *the*, will be lexically unmarked for this feature.

Once these lexical entries are in place, we can account for the phenomenon by treating nouns as follows. The SPR value of a count noun like *chair* would be ⟨D[COUNT +]⟩, forcing such nouns to co-occur with a count determiner. And the SPR value of a mass noun like *furniture* would be ⟨(D[COUNT −])⟩. As usual, the parentheses here designate optionality, and they appear only with mass nouns, because singular count nouns require determiners:[13]

(34) a.   (The) furniture is expensive.
      b.   The chair is expensive.
      c. *Chair is expensive.

Notice that under this analysis the feature COUNT is marked only on the determiners, not on the nouns themselves. (Hence COUNT is not an AGR feature, but rather a HEAD feature on a par with AGR.) Count and mass nouns are distinguished only by whether their SPR lists contain a [COUNT +] or [COUNT −] element. The matching of count nouns and count determiners is thus handled entirely by the Valence Principle and the Head-Specifier Rule, which will identify the SPR value

---

[13]This analysis of mass and plural nouns will be compared with an alternative in Problem 3 of Chapter 8.

of NOM (the head of the NP) and the category of its specifier. No new machinery need be introduced. Notice that this analysis also predicts that the COUNT specification is never passed up to the NP, and hence can never be selected by the VP. Thus there should be no verbs in English that require a count or mass subject or object.

Problem 3: COUNT and NUM
Is this last prediction right? That is, are there any verbs in English that require a count subject or object NP or a mass subject or object NP? Provide examples in support of your answer.

⚠ Problem 4: COUNT and NUM
An alternative to the analyses just presented would eliminate the feature COUNT and assign three values to the feature NUM: sg, pl, and mass. That is, mass nouns like *furniture* would be given the value [NUM mass]. Use the following data to provide an argument favoring the analysis given in the text over this alternative:

(i)   We don't have much $\left\{ \begin{array}{l} \text{rice} \\ \text{oats} \end{array} \right\}$.

(ii)* We don't have many $\left\{ \begin{array}{l} \text{rice} \\ \text{oats} \end{array} \right\}$.

(iii) The rice is in the bowl.
(iv)* The rice are in the bowl.
 (v) The oats are in the bowl.
(vi)* The oats is in the bowl.

[*Note: You may speak a variety of English that accepts many oats as a well-formed NP. There are some other nouns that are like oats in the relevant respects in at least some dialects, including grits (as a kind of cereal), mashed potatoes, and (somewhat distastefully, but grammatically more clearly) feces. If you can find a noun that patterns as we claim oats does in examples (i)–(vi), work the problem using that noun. If your dialect has no such nouns, then work the problem for the dialect described here, putting aside your own judgments.*]

The picture we now have of head-specifier structures is summarized in (35).

(35)

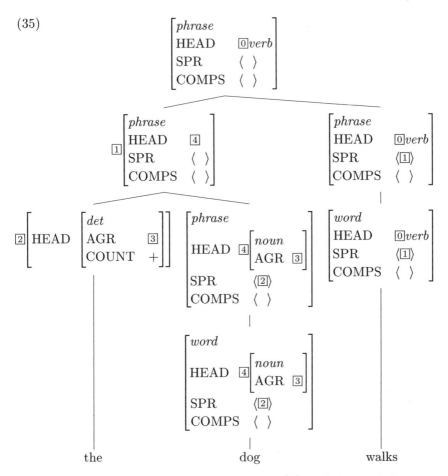

the   dog   walks

Note that the HEAD value of the noun *dog* (④) and those of the two
phrases above it are unified in virtue of the HFP. Similarly, the HFP
guarantees that the HEAD value of the verb *walks* (⓪) and those of the
two phrases above it are unified. The NSA guarantees that the AGR
value of the noun (③) is unified with that of the determiner it selects
as a specifier (②), and since the AGR specification is within the HEAD
value ④, it follows from the interaction of the NSA and the HFP that
the AGR values of the NP, NOM, N, and determiner in (35) are all
unified. This means in turn that whenever a verb selects a certain kind
of subject NP (an [AGR *3sing*] NP in the case of the verb *walks* in (35),
that selection will restrict what kind of noun and determiner can occur
within the subject NP, as desired.

4.8 Worksection on Case Marking

We close this chapter with a series of problems dealing with grammatical case. The tools developed in this chapter should suffice to provide an analysis of the phenomenon of case, in a manner analogous to the treatment of agreement.

4.8.1 Case Marking in English

Consider the following data:

(36) a. Dogs like him.
     b. *Dogs like he.
     c. *Him likes dogs.
     d. He likes dogs.

These sentences exemplify what linguists call CASE MARKING: *him* is what is called an ACCUSATIVE (or OBJECTIVE) case pronoun, and *he* is in what is called the NOMINATIVE (or SUBJECTIVE) case.

For the following problems, assume that there is a feature CASE with the values 'acc' and 'nom', and assume that English pronouns have CASE values specified in their lexical entries.

⚠ Problem 5: Assessing the Facts

As noted in Chapter 2, NPs appear in a variety of positions in English, including subject of a sentence, direct object of a verb, second object of a ditransitive verb like *give*, and object of a preposition. For each of these NP positions, determine which case the pronouns in that position must have. Give examples to support your claims.

⚠ Problem 6: A Lexical Analysis

In Chapter 2, problem 6 asked you to write phrase structure rules that would account for the different case markings associated with different positions in English. This kind of analysis of case marking no longer makes much sense, because we have replaced the very specific phrase structure rules of earlier chapters with more general rule schemas. Instead, we can now handle case entirely in the lexicon, without changing our grammar rules. Show how this could be done.

[*Hint: It will involve modifying the lexical entries of elements that combine with NPs.*]

Problem 7: Case and Coordination
There is considerable variation among English speakers about case marking in coordinate NPs. Consult your own intuitions (or those of a friend, if you are not a native English speaker) to determine what rule you use to assign case to pronouns in coordinate structures. State the rule informally – that is, give a succinct statement, in English, of a generalization that covers case in coordinate NPs in your dialect. Provide both grammatical and ungrammatical examples in support of your rule.

4.8.2 Case Marking in Icelandic

Icelandic is closely related to English, but it has a much more elaborate and interesting case system. For one thing, it has four cases: nominative, accusative, genitive, and dative. Second, case is marked not just on pronouns, but also on nouns. A third difference is illustrated in the following examples:[14]

(37) a. *Drengurinn kyssti stúlkuna.*
the-boy-NOM kissed the-girl-ACC
'The boy kissed the girl'

b. *Drengina   vantar mat.*
the-boys-ACC lacks   food-ACC
'The boys lack food'

c. *Verkjanna   gætir   ekki.*
the-pains-GEN is-noticeable not
'The pains are not noticeable'

d. *Barninu   batnaði   veikin*
the-child-DAT recovered-from the-disease-NOM
'The child recovered from the disease'

The case markings indicated in these examples are obligatory. Thus, for example, the following is ungrammatical because the subject should be accusative:

(38) **Drengurinn   vantar mat*
the-boy-NOM lacks   food-ACC

---

[14]In the glosses, NOM stands for 'nominative', ACC for 'accusative', GEN for 'genitive', and DAT for 'dative'. Although it may not be obvious from these examples, there is in fact ample evidence (which we cannot present here) that the initial NPs in these examples are the subjects of the verbs that follow them.

Problem 8: Choosing Analyses in Icelandic

Explain how the examples in (37) bear on the analysis of case marking in Icelandic. In particular, explain how they provide direct empirical evidence for treating case marking as a lexical phenomenon, rather than one associated with particular phrase structure positions. Be sure to sketch the lexical entry for at least one of these verbs.

4.8.3 Agreement and Case Marking in Wambaya

In Wambaya, a language of Northern Australia, nouns are divided into four genders: masculine (m), feminine (f), vegetable (v), and neuter (n). They are also inflected for case, such as ergative (E) and accusative (A). Consider the following Wambaya sentences, paying attention only to the agreement between the determiners and the nouns (you do not have to worry about accounting for, or understanding, the internal structure of these words or anything else in the sentence).[15]

(39) (i) *Ngankiyaga bungmanyani ngiya-ngajbi yaniyaga darranggu*
　　　 that.f.E　　 woman.f.E　　 she-saw　　 that.n.A　 tree.n.A
　　　 'That woman saw that tree'

　　 (ii) *Ngankiyaga bungmanyani ngiya-ngajbi mamiyaga jigama*
　　　 that.f.E　　 woman.f.E　　 she-saw　　 that.v.A　 yam.v.A
　　　 'That woman saw that yam'

　　 (iii) *Ngankiyaga bungmanyani ngiya-ngajbi iniyaga　 bungmaji*
　　　 that.f.E　　 woman.f.E　　 she-saw　　 that.m.A　 man.m.A
　　　 'That woman saw that man'

　　 (iv) *Ninkiyaga bungmanyini gina-ngajbi naniyaga bungmanya*
　　　 that.m.E　 man.m.E　　 he-saw　　 that.f.A　 woman.f.A
　　　 'That man saw that woman'

　　 (v) *Ninkiyaga bungmanyini gina-ngajbi yaniyaga darranggu*
　　　 that.m.E　 man.m.E　　 he-saw　　 that.n.A　 tree.n.A
　　　 'That man saw that tree'

　　 (vi) *Ninkiyaga bungmanyini gina-ngajbi mamiyaga jigama*
　　　 that.m.E　 man.m.E　　 he-saw　　 that.v.A　 yam.v.A
　　　 'That man saw that yam'

---

[15]In fact, the Wambaya data presented here are simplified in various ways: only one of the numerous word-order patterns is illustrated and the auxiliary plus verb sequences (e.g. *ngiya-ngajbi*) are here presented as a single word, when in fact the auxiliary is an independent verb in 'second' position. We are grateful to Rachel Nordlinger, who constructed this problem, in addition to conducting the field work upon which it is based.

Ergative is the standard name for the case of the subject of a transitive verb in languages like Wambaya, where intransitive and transitive subjects show different inflection patterns. Nothing crucial in this problem hinges on the distinction between nominative and ergative case. Note that the agreement patterns in (39) are the only ones possible; for example, changing *mamiyaga* to *yaniyaga* in (vi) would be ungrammatical. Note also that the verbs are selecting for the case of the subject and object NPs, so, for example, *gina-ngajbi* must take an ergative subject and accusative object.

Problem 9: Analyzing Case in Wambaya

    A. Since verbs select subjects and objects of a particular case and this case shows up in terms of the inflection of the head noun, what does this illustrate (minimally) about the feature CASE (i.e. where must it go in our feature geometry)?

    B. Explain how our analysis of English determiner-noun agreement would have to be modified in order to account for Wambaya determiner-noun agreement.

    C. Illustrate your analysis with lexical entries for *bungmanyani*, *ngankiyaga*, *bungmaji*, and *iniyaga*.

4.9 Summary

In the previous chapter, we had already seen that cross-categorial generalizations about phrase structure can be expressed in terms of schematic phrase structure rules and categories specified in terms of feature structures. In this chapter, the real power of feature structure grammars has begun to emerge. We have begun the process of providing a unified account of the generalizations about complementation and specifier selection, in terms of the list-valued features COMPS and SPR. These features, together with the Valence Principle, have enabled us to eliminate further redundancy from our grammar rules. In fact, our grammar has now been reduced to the following four very general rules:

(40) a. Head-Specifier Rule

$$\begin{bmatrix} phrase \\ \text{SPR} \quad \langle\,\rangle \end{bmatrix} \rightarrow \boxed{1} \quad \text{H}\begin{bmatrix} phrase \\ \text{SPR} \quad \langle\,\boxed{1}\,\rangle \end{bmatrix}$$

b. Head-Complement Rule

$$\begin{bmatrix} phrase \\ \text{COMPS} \quad \langle \ \rangle \end{bmatrix} \rightarrow \text{H}\begin{bmatrix} word \\ \text{COMPS} \quad \langle \boxed{1},...,\boxed{n} \rangle \end{bmatrix} \boxed{1} \ ... \ \boxed{n}$$

c. Head-Modifier Rule

$$\begin{bmatrix} phrase \end{bmatrix} \rightarrow \text{H}\begin{bmatrix} phrase \end{bmatrix} \text{PP}[...]$$

d. Coordination Rule

$$\boxed{1} \rightarrow \boxed{1}^{+} \quad \text{CONJ} \quad \boxed{1}$$

Moreover, we have seen in this chapter that key generalizations about agreement and case marking can also be expressed in terms of this highly compact rule system, once we rely on categories modeled as feature structures.

4.10 Further Reading

The idea of schematizing phrase structure rules across parts of speech was introduced into generative grammar by Chomsky (1970). For a variety of perspectives on grammatical agreement, see Barlow and Ferguson (1988). A helpful discussion of Icelandic case is provided by Andrews (1982).

5

Semantics

5.1 Introduction

Before we can return to the distribution of reflexive and nonreflexive pronouns, which will be the topic of Chapter 7, we need to consider the nature of reference and coreference – topics that are fundamentally semantic in nature (i.e. that have to do in large part with meaning). And before we can do that, we need to discuss meaning more generally and to sketch how meaning will be represented in our grammar.

Reflexive pronouns provide perhaps the clearest case in which a semantic factor – coreference, in this case – plays an essential role in the grammatical distribution of particular words. But there are many other syntactic phenomena that are closely linked to meaning. Consider, for example, subject-verb agreement, which we have discussed extensively in the past two chapters. Singular nouns generally refer to individual objects, and plural nouns normally refer to collections of objects. Mass nouns usually refer to substances – that is, entities that are not naturally packaged into discrete objects. Of course, how objects, collections, and substances are individuated is not fully determined by the structure of the world, so there may be differences between languages, or even between individuals in how things are referred to. Hence the German word *Hose* means essentially the same thing as English *pants* or *trousers*, but the German is singular while the English is plural. Likewise, individual English speakers differ as to whether they can use *lettuce* as a count noun. Syntactic properties (including such basic ones as the part-of-speech distinctions) are often closely linked to semantic characteristics, though the correspondences are usually imperfect. Trying to do syntax without acknowledging the associated semantic regularities would lead to missing many fundamental generalizations about linguistic structure.

The study of meaning is even older than the study of grammar, and there is little hope of doing justice to problems of semantics in a textbook whose primary concern is grammatical structure. However, if the study of grammar is going to play any role in modeling real language use, then grammar minimally has to include an analysis of the meaning of individual words and a treatment of how these combine with each other – that is, an account of how meanings of phrases and sentences are built up from the meanings of their parts. So let us begin by contemplating the nature of sentence meaning.

5.2 Semantics and Pragmatics

Meaning is inextricably bound up with actions – people use language intentionally for many kinds of communicative purposes. Some sentences are used to convey questions; others simple assertions; still others conventionally convey commands (or 'directives', as they are sometimes called). Even a piece of a sentence, say an NP like *the student sitting behind Leslie*, can be used in isolation to perform a simple act of referring to an individual.

The kind of meaning that (a particular use of) a sentence conventionally conveys depends crucially on its syntactic form. For example, a simple 'inverted' sentence like (1), with an auxiliary verb before the subject NP, conventionally conveys a question.

(1) Is Sandy tall?

And the question posed by (1) is closely related to the proposition that is asserted by an utterance of the noninverted sentence in (2).

(2) Sandy is tall.

In fact, uttering (2) is a perfectly good way of answering (1).

To even begin to deal with semantic problems such as these, we first have to clarify what the units of meaning are and how particular kinds of sentences or smaller phrases are tied to particular types of meaning by linguistic conventions. We will make what is a standard assumption, that communication has two components: linguistic meaning and reasoning about communicative goals. On this view, when a linguistic expression is uttered, its linguistic meaning makes a significant contribution to, but does not fully determine, the communicative function of the utterance. Consider, for example, an utterance of (3).

(3) Do you have a quarter?

The linguistic meaning of this sentence is a familiar kind of semantic object: a question. And a question of this form has a determinate answer: yes or no. However, an utterance of (3) might serve to communicate much more than such a simple factual inquiry. In particular, in addition to posing a financial question to a given hearer, an utterance of (3) is likely to convey a further message – that the speaker was making the following request of the addressee.

(4) Please give me a quarter!

The question conveyed by an utterance of (3) is generally referred to as its LITERAL or CONVENTIONAL meaning. A request like (4) is communicated as a further message above and beyond the message expressed by the literal meaning of the question in (3). We will leave the account of such embellished communication (even the routine 'reading between the lines' that occurs more or less effortlessly in cases like this) to a more fully developed theory of language use, that is, to a theory of linguistic PRAGMATICS. The inference from question to request is a pragmatic one.

By contrast, the fact that a sentence like (3) must express a question as its literal meaning is semantic in nature. SEMANTICS is the study of linguistic meaning, that is, the contribution to communication that derives directly from the conventions of the language. Pragmatics is a more general study, of how linguistic meaning interacts with situational factors and the plans and goals of conversational participants to achieve more subtle, often elaborate communicative effects.

The semantic analysis that a grammar provides serves as input for a theory of pragmatics or language use. Such a theory sets as its goal to explain what actually gets communicated via pragmatic inferences derived from the linguistic meaning of an utterance. For example, pragmatic theory might include a principle like (5):[1]

(5) Quantity Principle (simplified)

     If X is weaker than Y, then asserting X implies the denial of Y.

This principle leads to pragmatic inference via 'proofs' of the following kind (justifications for steps of the proof are given in parentheses):

(6)   • A says to B: *Two things bother Pat.*
       • A uttered something whose linguistic meaning is:
         'Two things bother Pat'. (semantic analysis)
       • 'Two things bother Pat'. is weaker than 'Three things bother
         Pat'. (This is true in the context; possibly true more gener-
         ally)

---

[1]The principle in (5), due to Grice (1989), relies on the undefined term 'weaker'. In some cases (such as the example that follows), it is intuitively obvious what 'weaker' means. But a full-fledged pragmatic theory that included (5) would have to provide a precise definition of this term.

- B assumes that A also meant to communicate: 'It's not the case that three things bother Pat'. (Quantity Principle)

Note that exactly the same pragmatic inference would arise from an utterance by A of any semantically equivalent sentence, such as *There are two things that bother Pat* or *Pat is bothered by two things*. This is because pragmatic theory works from the linguistic meaning of an utterance (as characterized by our semantic analysis) and hence is indifferent to the form by which such meanings are expressed.[2]

There is much more that could be said about the fascinating topic of pragmatic inference. Here, the only purpose has been to show that the semantic analysis that must be included in any adequate grammar plays an essential role, albeit an indirect one, in explaining the communicative function of language in context.

5.3 Linguistic Meaning

5.3.1 Kinds of Meaning

When we ask a question, make an assertion, or even issue a command, we are also making reference to something that is often called a SIT-UATION or EVENT.[3] If you utter a sentence like *Kim is running*, for example, you assert that there is some running situation in the world that involves something (usually a person) named Kim. The proposition that you assert is either true or false depending on a number of things, for example, whether this situation is a running event (maybe Kim is moving too slowly for it to really qualify as running), or whether the runner is someone named Kim (maybe the person you have in mind is really Leslie), whether the running situation is really happening now (maybe Kim has already run the race but my watch stopped several hours ago). If any of these 'maybes' turns out to be the case, then what you have said is false – the situation you are describing as specified by the linguistic meaning of the sentence is not part of the real world.

---

[2]This is not quite true. Sometimes the manner in which something is said (the form of an utterance) can make some pragmatic contribution to an utterance, but a discussion of such cases would take us too far afield.

[3]Although the term 'event' is often used in a general sense in semantic discussions, this terminology can be misleading, especially in connection with circumstances like the following, where nothing very event-like is happening:

(i) Bo knows baseball.
(ii) Dana is aggressive.
(iii) Sydney resembles Terry.
(iv) Chris is tall.
(v) 37 is a prime number.

We find it much more intuitive to discuss such sentences in terms of 'situations' and hence have adopted this as our official terminology for the semantics of sentences.

An important part of the business of semantics is specifying truth conditions such as these, that is, specifying restrictions which must be satisfied by particular situations in order for assertions about them to be true. And since truth conditions are determined in large part by linguistic meaning, our grammar will be incomplete unless we introduce (i) some way of representing the linguistic meanings of words and (ii) a set of constraints that allows us to correctly predict the linguistic meanings of phrase structures in terms of the meanings of their parts (their subconstituents).

Consider what this means in the case of *Kim is running*. What we need to guarantee is that this sentence gets a semantics that is a proposition (not a question or a directive, for example) specified in terms of the following conditions:[4]

(7) a. there is a situation s
     b. s is a running situation
     c. the runner is some individual i
     d. i is named Kim
     e. s is temporally located around the time of utterance

If there is some situation s and some individual i such that all the conditions in (7) are satisfied, then the proposition expressed by *Kim is running* is true. If not, then that proposition is false.

So to take care of semantic business, we will need a way to ensure that the various pieces of this sentence – the noun *Kim*, the verb *is*, and the verb *running* – each make its appropriate contribution to the set of constraints summarized in (7) and that the grammar specifies how such propositions are built up from the substructures of the sentence. Our account must also be sufficiently general so as to assign the correct semantic description to all sentences of the language. So for example, a sentence like *Is Kim running?* should be assigned a semantics of a different type – that of a question – but a question about whether or not there is a situation s and an individual i such that all the conditions in (7) are satisfied.

In this book, we will construct meaning descriptions by providing constraints that specify how a phrase's semantics is built up from the semantics of its immediate constituents. Our method for predicting the semantics of a given phrase will thus be the same as our method of constraining the syntactic feature specifications of the mother node

---

[4]The exact meaning of the progressive (*be...-ing*) construction is a fascinating semantic topic with a considerable literature that we cannot do justice to here. We have adopted clause (7e) as a convenient first approximation of the truth conditional contribution of the present progressive in English.

in a phrase structure: in terms of general constraints that determine how the mother's value for a given feature is related to the daughters' specifications for the same feature.

The semantic objects of our grammar will be classified in terms of four SEMANTIC MODES – that is, the four basic kinds of meanings that are enumerated and illustrated in (8).

(8)

SEMANTIC MODE	KIND OF PHRASE	EXAMPLE
proposition	noninverted sentence	Kim is happy.
question	inverted sentence	Is Kim happy?
directive	imperative phrase	Be happy!
reference	NP	Palo Alto

To achieve this classification, we will represent the meanings of all kinds of linguistic expressions in terms of feature structures that specify three things: a semantic mode, an index corresponding to the situation or individual referred to, and a restriction (abbreviated 'RESTR') specifying a list of conditions that the situation or individual has to satisfy for the expression to be applicable to it. Semantic structures then will look like (9):

$$(9) \quad \begin{bmatrix} \text{MODE} \\ \text{INDEX} \\ \text{RESTR} \end{bmatrix}$$

The feature INDEX differs from other features we have encountered, in that it can take an unlimited number of different atomic values. This is because there is no limit to the number of different individuals or situations which can be referred to in a single sentence. Consequently, we must have an unbounded number of values of INDEX available. These atomic values of INDEX will conventionally be written with lower-case Roman letters; instead of tagging two occurrences of the same INDEX value, we will simply write the same index (that is, the same lower-case Roman letter) in both places.

Propositions are analyzed in terms of feature structures like the one in (10) (where 'prop' is short for 'proposition').

$$(10) \quad \begin{bmatrix} \text{MODE} & \text{prop} \\ \text{INDEX} & s \\ \text{RESTR} & \langle \dots \rangle \end{bmatrix}$$

A proposition like (10) will be true just in case there is some actual situation s (and there exist appropriate other individuals corresponding to

whatever variables are present in (10)) such that the constraints specified in the RESTR value of (10) are all satisfied. These restrictions,
the nature of which will be explained in the next section, must include
all those that are relevant to the meaning of the sentence, for example,
all the constraints just mentioned in conjunction with the truth or fal-
sity of *Kim is running*. Our grammatical analysis must ensure that we
end up with exactly the right constraints in the RESTR list of a sentence's semantics, so that we associate exactly the right meaning with
any sentence sanctioned by our grammar.

Questions and directives have a similar analysis, though the intuition
behind their meaning is somewhat different. A question like *Is Kim
running?* must be assigned a semantics just like the one assigned to
Kim is running, except that the MODE value must be 'question' ('ques'
for short), rather than 'prop':

(11)
$$\begin{bmatrix} \text{MODE} & \text{ques} \\ \text{INDEX} & s \\ \text{RESTR} & \langle \dots \rangle \end{bmatrix}$$

The question of whether a situation s satisfies a set of restrictions is the
kind of semantic object that can be resolved positively or negatively in
a given context, though it is not itself true or false. We can thus talk of
true or false answers to questions, but questions themselves are neither
true nor false.

Neither are directives ('dir' for short), which are represented as in
(12).

(12)
$$\begin{bmatrix} \text{MODE} & \text{dir} \\ \text{INDEX} & s \\ \text{RESTR} & \langle \dots \rangle \end{bmatrix}$$

A directive – for example, *Shut the door* – is rather something that can be
fulfilled or not; and what the RESTR list does in the case of a directive
is to specify what conditions have to be satisfied in order for a directive
to be fulfilled.

A reference ('ref' for short) is similar to the kinds of meanings just
illustrated, except that it can be used to pick out (or DENOTE) all kinds
of entities – not just situations. We use INDICES notated with the letters
i, j, k, etc. as the INDEX values for the semantics of nominal expressions. These function much in the same way as variables in algebra or in
mathematical logic. The INDEX values written with the letters s, t, u,
etc. are for indices that refer only to situations. Other indices are free

to be associated with any kind of entity found in a discourse context.[5] So the semantics we assign to a referring NP has the following form:

(13)
$$\begin{bmatrix} \text{MODE} & \text{ref} \\ \text{INDEX} & i \\ \text{RESTR} & \langle \, ... \, \rangle \end{bmatrix}$$

As we have just seen, there are a number of differences among the various semantic modes we have assumed. Despite these differences, the modes have something in common. Every kind of linguistic expression we have considered, irrespective of its semantic mode, refers to something that must satisfy an indicated list of restrictions for the expression to be correctly applicable. Our approach to semantics expresses this general fact by treating all expressions in terms of a single type of semantic object that includes a referential index of one kind or another. The semantic work of distinguishing the ways in which the individuals and situations referred to contribute to linguistic meaning is left to the differing values of the feature MODE. Many words and phrases that cannot be used by themselves to express a proposition, ask a question, refer to an individual, etc. (e.g. determiners, prepositions, PPs, and conjunctions) will be treated here in terms of the specification [MODE none].

5.3.2 Predications

The goal of semantics is to account for the systematic role of linguistic meaning in communication. As we have just seen, we can approach this goal in terms of a semantic analysis that recognizes diverse semantic modes and reference to both individuals and situations. Much of the interesting work in linguistic semantics is done by the conditions associated with particular linguistic expressions, conditions which situations and individuals must meet in order for those expressions to be applicable to them. In terms of our analysis, this means that it will be particularly important how individual words contribute to the values of the feature RESTR, and how the RESTR values of phrases are built up from those of their parts.

Semantic restrictions associated with expressions come in many varieties, which concern what properties some individual has, who did what to whom in some situation, when, where, or why some situation occurred, and so forth. That is, semantically relevant restrictions specify which of the properties must hold of individuals and situations, and

---

[5]There are any number of intriguing referential puzzles that are the subject of ongoing inquiry by semanticists. For example, what does an NP like *a page* refer to in the sentence: *A page is missing from this book?* Or *the unicorn that Chris is looking for* in the sentence: *The unicorn that Chris is looking for doesn't exist?*

which relations must hold among them, for an expression to be applicable.

To represent this sort of information, we must introduce into our semantics some way of specifying relations among entities quite generally. We do this by introducing a type of feature structure called *predication* (*pred*). The features of a predication specify (i) what kind of relation is involved and (ii) who or what is participating in the relation. Examples of feature structures of type *pred* are given in (14).[6]

(14)   a.
$$
\begin{bmatrix}
\text{RELN} & \text{love} \\
\text{SIT(UATION)} & s \\
\text{LOVER} & i \\
\text{LOVED} & j
\end{bmatrix}
$$
b.
$$
\begin{bmatrix}
\text{RELN} & \text{walk} \\
\text{SIT} & s \\
\text{WALKER} & i
\end{bmatrix}
$$

c.
$$
\begin{bmatrix}
\text{RELN} & \text{give} \\
\text{SIT} & s \\
\text{GIVER} & i \\
\text{RECIPIENT} & j \\
\text{GIFT} & k
\end{bmatrix}
$$
d.
$$
\begin{bmatrix}
\text{RELN} & \text{book} \\
\text{SIT} & s \\
\text{INSTANCE} & k
\end{bmatrix}
$$

e.
$$
\begin{bmatrix}
\text{RELN} & \text{happy} \\
\text{SIT} & s \\
\text{INSTANCE} & i
\end{bmatrix}
$$
f.
$$
\begin{bmatrix}
\text{RELN} & \text{under} \\
\text{SIT} & s \\
\text{LOWER} & i \\
\text{HIGHER} & j
\end{bmatrix}
$$

The predications in (14) are meant to correspond to conditions such as: 's is a situation wherein i loves j', 's is a situation wherein i walks', 's is a situation wherein i gives k to j', 's is a situation wherein k is a book', 's is a situation wherein i is happy', and 's is a situation wherein i is under j', respectively. We will henceforth make frequent use of predications like these, without taking the time to present a proper theory of relations, predications, and the features that go with them.

---

[6]The kind of event-based semantic analysis we employ was pioneered by the philosopher Donald Davidson in a number of papers. (See, for example, Davidson (1980).) Our simplified representations differ from certain popular formulations where all talk of existence is represented via explicit existential quantification, i.e. in terms of representations like (i):

  (i) there is an event s and an individual i such that: s is a running event, the runner of s is i, i is named Kim, and s is temporally located around the time of utterance

We will treat all such existential quantification as implicit in our semantic descriptions.

Note that the restriction associated with many nouns and adjectives (*book*, *happy*, etc.) includes a predication of only one (nonsituation) argument. In such cases – for example, (14d,e) – we use the feature INST(ANCE).

Almost all words specify restrictions that involve predications of one kind or another, including verbs, adjectives, prepositions, and nouns. In order for phrases containing such words to inherit these restrictions, there must be constraints that (minimally) guarantee that the RESTR values of a phrase's daughters are part of that phrase's RESTR value. Only in this way will we end up with a sentence whose RESTR value includes all the necessary restrictions on the relevant event participants.

For example, for a simple sentence like (15), we will want a semantic description like the one sketched in (16).

(15) A girl saved a boy.

$$(16) \begin{bmatrix} \text{MODE} & \text{prop} \\ \text{INDEX} & s \\ \text{RESTR} & \left\langle \begin{bmatrix} \text{RELN} & \text{save} \\ \text{SIT} & s \\ \text{SAVER} & i \\ \text{SAVED} & j \end{bmatrix}, \begin{bmatrix} \text{RELN} & \text{girl} \\ \text{SIT} & t \\ \text{INST} & i \end{bmatrix}, \begin{bmatrix} \text{RELN} & \text{boy} \\ \text{SIT} & u \\ \text{INST} & j \end{bmatrix} \right\rangle \end{bmatrix}$$

The conditions on s come from the lexical entry for the verb *save*, the constraint that i – the saver – must be a girl comes from the noun *girl*, and the constraint that j – the saved (person) – must be a boy comes from the lexical entry for the noun *boy*. By associating (15) with the feature structure in (16), our semantic analysis says that the linguistic meaning of (15) is the proposition that will be true just in case there is an actual situation that involves the saving of a boy by a girl. But in order to produce the right set of conditions in the sentence's semantic description, the conditions of the parts of the sentence have to be amalgamated into a single list of conditions. Note in addition that the main situation of the sentence is derived from that introduced by the verb. It is true in general that the semantics of a phrase will crucially involve the semantics of its head daughter.

5.4 How Semantics Fits In

In earlier chapters, we considered only the syntactic properties of linguistic expressions. To accommodate the basic analysis of linguistic meaning just sketched, we need some way of introducing semantic structures into the feature structures we use to analyze words and phrases. We do this by adding two new features – SYN(TAX) and SEM(ANTICS) – and adding a level of embedding within our feature structures, as illustrated in (17):

(17)
$$
\begin{bmatrix}
\text{SYN} & \begin{bmatrix} \text{HEAD} & [...] \\ \text{SPR} & ... \\ \text{COMPS} & ... \end{bmatrix} \\
\text{SEM} & \begin{bmatrix} \text{MODE} & \\ \text{INDEX} & \\ \text{RESTR} & \langle\, ... \,\rangle \end{bmatrix}
\end{bmatrix}
$$

There is now a syntactic side and a semantic side to all feature structures like (17), which we will assign to the type called *synsem-struc(ture)*. Although we will add a few more features as we progress, this is in essence the feature geometry that we will adopt in the remainder of the book. We will frequently have occasion in what follows to refer to the synsem-struc of a phrase. What we mean by this is the full feature structure that is the top node of the SD of that phrase, including both its SYN and SEM values.

This changes the way lexical entries look, of course; and this is illustrated in (18):

(18) a.
$$
\left\langle \text{woman}\,, \begin{bmatrix}
\text{SYN} & \begin{bmatrix} \text{HEAD} & \begin{bmatrix} \textit{noun} \\ \text{AGR} & \boxed{1}\textit{3sing} \end{bmatrix} \\ \text{SPR} & \langle\, \text{Det[AGR } \boxed{1}] \,\rangle \\ \text{COMPS} & \langle\,\rangle \end{bmatrix} \\
\text{SEM} & \begin{bmatrix} \text{MODE} & \text{ref} \\ \text{INDEX} & i \\ \text{RESTR} & \left\langle \begin{bmatrix} \text{RELN} & \text{woman} \\ \text{SIT} & s \\ \text{INST} & i \end{bmatrix} \right\rangle \end{bmatrix}
\end{bmatrix} \right\rangle
$$

b.

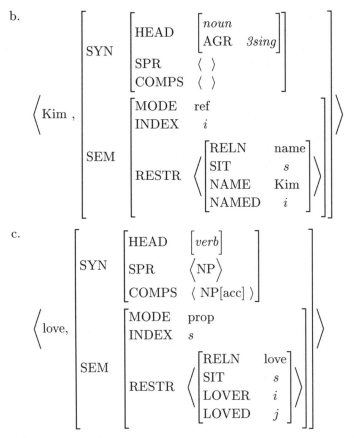

c.

It should be noted that our semantic analysis of proper names (one of many that have been proposed over the centuries) treats them as simple referring expressions whose referent must be appropriately named.[7] Under our assumption that all NPs[8] have an index as their INDEX value, it is straightforward to associate the semantics of NPs with the particular roles they play in a verb's predication. We shall assume that the role arguments within predications are indices, and hence we can achieve the desired result by letting a verb (and other elements with predicational semantics) specify links between the indices of its dependents (specifiers and complements) and the role arguments in the predication on the RE-

---

[7]In a more precise account, we might add the further condition that the speaker intend to refer to the referent. Under this analysis, a sentence like *Kim walks* would be regarded as true just in case there is a walking event involving a certain individual that the speaker intends to refer to and who is named 'Kim'.

[8]Except 'dummy' NPs like *there*, which we will turn to in Chapter 11.

STR list of its own semantics. This is illustrated in (19) for the verb
love.

> *NB: Here and throughout, we use NP$_i$ as a shorthand for an NP
> whose SEM value's INDEX is i.*

(19)

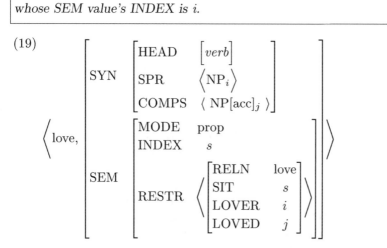

In this way, as the verb combines with a particular NP object, the index
of that NP is identified with the value of the feature LOVED in the
verb's semantics. The verb's INDEX value is identified with that of the
VP it heads, and the verb's restrictions are included in the VP's RESTR
value, so that when that VP combines with the subject, the identities
specified in (19) will also guarantee that the index of the actual subject
of the sentence will be the LOVER in the loving predication on the
VP's RESTR list. This will in turn be included in the RESTR value
of the S, by the Semantic Compositionality Principle (introduced later
in this chapter) which requires that the mother's RESTR list include
all the RESTR lists of its daughters. Hence the unifications specified in
(19) ensure that the conditions specified by the sentence's subject and
object are those conditions about the lover and loved participants in the
predication that involves the situation that the sentence as a whole is
about.

We will illustrate how the SEM value of a complex expression relates
to its parts in more detail in section 5.6. Before concluding this section,
however, we must point out that we are glossing over one important
issue (among others) in our cursory presentation of semantic analysis.
This is the matter of quantification. Sentences like those in (20) require
a semantic treatment that goes beyond simple reference to individuals.

(20) a. Everyone liked *Sense and Sensibility.*

    b. Most people are reading a book by Austen.

    c. Few people who have met you say there is nothing unusual about you.

The approach to NP semantics sketched here can easily be extended to deal with sentences containing quantified NPs (*everyone, most people*, etc.), by augmenting our feature structures to allow more complex propositions (as well as questions and directives) that represent quantification over individuals explicitly (in terms of 'binding' of indices). We will leave this entire topic unexplored here, however, noting only that it is possible to introduce explicit quantification over situations as well.

5.5   Modification

Suppose that we introduce a HEAD feature called MOD and that the MOD value of a word specifies the kind of thing the word modifies. Then we could make it a lexical property of adjectives that they were [MOD NOM] (or [MOD NP]) and a lexical property of adverbs that they were [MOD VP] (or [MOD S]). Since these modifiers would then 'pass up' their MOD value, courtesy of the Head Feature Principle, to any phrase that they projected (i.e. that they were the head daughter of), it would then be possible to use a single Head-Modifier Rule, as in (21), to account for both nominal and verbal modification.

(21) Head-Modifier Rule

$$[\textit{phrase}] \; \rightarrow \; \text{H}\boxed{1}[\textit{phrase}] \; \begin{bmatrix} \textit{phrase} \\ \text{HEAD } [\text{MOD } \boxed{1}] \end{bmatrix}$$

That is, rule (21) will license a NOM just in case the head daughter is a phrase of category NOM and the modifier daughter's MOD value is also of category NOM:

(22)

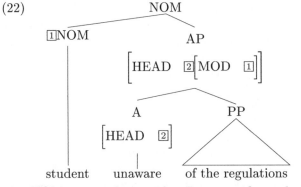

This NOM can combine with a D as specifier to build an NP like (23):

(23) a student unaware of the regulations

The Head-Modifier Rule in (21) will also license the verb phrase in (24), under the assumption that adverbs are lexically specified as [MOD VP].[9]

(24)

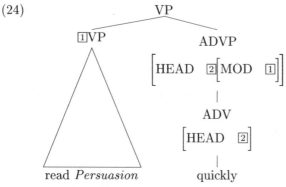

$$
\begin{array}{c}
\text{VP} \\
\diagup\quad\diagdown \\
\boxed{1}\text{VP}\qquad\qquad \text{ADVP} \\
\left[\text{HEAD}\ \boxed{2}\left[\text{MOD}\ \boxed{1}\right]\right] \\
| \\
\text{ADV} \\
\left[\text{HEAD}\ \boxed{2}\right] \\
|
\end{array}
$$

read *Persuasion*   quickly

And a VP satisfying this description can combine with a subject like the one in (23) to build sentence (25).

(25) A student unaware of the regulations read *Persuasion* quickly.

Note further that many prepositional phrase modifiers can modify either nominal or verbal constituents:

(26) a. The [reporter [in Rome]]...
     b. We [went shopping [in Rome]]

(27) a. The [weather [on Sunday]]...
     b. We [went shopping [on Sunday]]

The bare bones treatment of modification just sketched can easily account for these examples by allowing underspecified or disjunctively specified MOD values for such prepositions.

5.6 The Semantic Principles

We are now not only able to analyze the form of sentences of considerable complexity using our grammar, but in addition we can analyze the meanings of complex sentences by adding semantic constraints on the structures defined by our rules. The most general of these semantic constraints is given in (28):

---

[9]We assume here that there is a lexical category (a subtype of *part-of-speech*) for adverbs (ADV). The Head-Complement Rule then licenses adverb phrases (ADVP). We do not examine the syntax of adverb phrases in any detail in this text.

(28) Semantic Compositionality Principle

In any well-formed phrase structure, the mother's RESTR value is the sum of the RESTR values of the daughters.

In other words, all restrictions from all the daughters in a phrase are collected into the RESTR value of the mother. The term 'sum' has a straightforward meaning here: the sum of the RESTR values of the daughters is the list whose members are those values, taken in order.[10] We will use the symbol '⊕' to designate the sum operator.[11]

In addition to the Semantic Compositionality Principle, we introduce the following constraint on the MODE and INDEX values of headed phrases:

(29) Semantic Inheritance Principle

In any headed phrase, the mother's MODE and INDEX values are identical to those of the head daughter.

The Semantic Inheritance Principle guarantees that the semantic MODE and INDEX of a phrase are identified with those of the head daughter, giving the semantics, like the syntax, a 'head-driven' character.

The effect of these two semantic principles is illustrated in the simple example, (30). The effect of both semantic principles can be clearly observed in the S node at the top of this SD. The MODE is 'prop', inherited from its head daughter, the VP node, (and ultimately from the head verb, *aches*) by the Semantic Inheritance Principle. In this same way, the INDEX value 's' comes from the verb, through the VP. The RESTR value of the S node, [RESTR ⟨ ③ , ④ ⟩], is the sum of the RESTR values of the NP and VP nodes, as specified by the Semantic Compositionality Principle.

Note that here, as before, we use abbreviations like 'NP', 'S', and 'V' to abbreviate feature structure descriptions specifying purely syntactic information. Since the labels of nodes in phrasal SDs will now include semantic information, the notational abbreviations should henceforth be reinterpreted accordingly (as standing for entire synsem-strucs).

With these semantic principles in place, we can now complete our account of modification. Let us assume that an adverb like *today* has a lexical entry like the one in (31).

---

[10]That is, the sum of lists ⟨ A ⟩, ⟨ B, C ⟩, and ⟨ D ⟩ is the list ⟨ A, B, C, D ⟩.

[11]Notice that, unlike the familiar arithmetic sum operator, ⊕ is not commutative: ⟨ A ⟩ ⊕ ⟨ B ⟩ = ⟨ A, B ⟩, but ⟨ B ⟩ ⊕ ⟨ A ⟩ = ⟨ B, A ⟩. And ⟨ A, B ⟩ ≠ ⟨ B, A ⟩, because the order of the elements matters. Although the order of elements in RESTR lists has no semantic significance, the relative ordering of elements in the ARG-ST lists that we construct using ⊕ in Chapter 7 is crucial to our account of reflexive binding.

(30)

S

$$\begin{bmatrix} phrase \\ \text{SPR} & \langle\ \rangle \\ \text{MODE} & \text{prop} \\ \text{INDEX} & s \\ \text{RESTR} & \langle\ \boxed{3},\ \boxed{4}\ \rangle \end{bmatrix}$$

$\boxed{1}$NP

$$\begin{bmatrix} phrase \\ \text{MODE} & \text{ref} \\ \text{INDEX} & i \\ \text{RESTR} & \langle\boxed{3}\rangle \end{bmatrix}$$

VP

$$\begin{bmatrix} phrase \\ \text{SPR} & \langle\boxed{1}\rangle \\ \text{MODE} & \text{prop} \\ \text{INDEX} & s \\ \text{RESTR} & \langle\boxed{4}\rangle \end{bmatrix}$$

N

$$\begin{bmatrix} word \\ \text{MODE} & \text{ref} \\ \text{INDEX} & i \\ \\ \text{RESTR} & \left\langle\ \boxed{3}\begin{bmatrix} \text{RELN} & \text{name} \\ \text{SIT} & t \\ \text{NAME} & \text{Pat} \\ \text{NAMED} & i \end{bmatrix}\right\rangle \end{bmatrix}$$

V

$$\begin{bmatrix} word \\ \text{SPR} & \langle\boxed{1}\text{NP}_i\rangle \\ \text{MODE} & \text{prop} \\ \text{INDEX} & s \\ \\ \text{RESTR} & \left\langle\ \boxed{4}\begin{bmatrix} \text{RELN} & \text{ache} \\ \text{SIT} & s \\ \text{ACHER} & i \end{bmatrix}\right\rangle \end{bmatrix}$$

Pat

aches

(31)

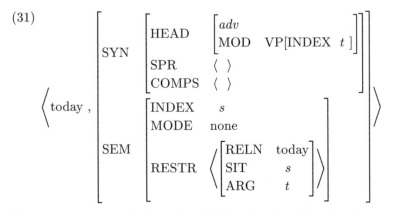

$$\left\langle \text{today}, \begin{bmatrix} \text{SYN} & \begin{bmatrix} \text{HEAD} & \begin{bmatrix} adv \\ \text{MOD} & \text{VP[INDEX } t\,] \end{bmatrix} \\ \text{SPR} & \langle\,\rangle \\ \text{COMPS} & \langle\,\rangle \end{bmatrix} \\ \text{SEM} & \begin{bmatrix} \text{INDEX} & s \\ \text{MODE} & \text{none} \\ \text{RESTR} & \left\langle \begin{bmatrix} \text{RELN} & \text{today} \\ \text{SIT} & s \\ \text{ARG} & t \end{bmatrix} \right\rangle \end{bmatrix} \end{bmatrix} \right\rangle$$

The key point here is that the MOD value identifies the index of the VP to be modified as 't', the same situation that is the argument of the relation 'today' in the semantic restriction. This means that once the adverb combines with a VP, the (situational) index of that VP is the argument of 'today'.[12]

Our two semantic principles, the Head-Modifier Rule, and the lexical entry in (31) thus interact to define SDs like (32) (only SEM values are indicated). In this way, our analysis provides a general account of how meanings are constructed. The Semantic Compositionality Principle and the Semantic Inheritance Principle together embody a simple yet powerful theory of the relation between the structures of our grammar and the meanings they convey.

5.7 Coordination Revisited

The analysis of the previous section specifies how meanings are associated with the headed structures of our grammar, by placing appropriate constraints on those phrasal SDs that result from our headed rules. It also covers the composition of the RESTR values in nonheaded rules. But nothing in the previous discussion specifies the MODE or INDEX values of coordinate phrases – the one kind of phrase licensed by the Coordination Rule, a nonheaded rule.

---

[12]It would be equivalent to use tags when identifying indices, e.g. as in (i):

(i) $\begin{bmatrix} \text{INDEX} & \boxed{1}s \end{bmatrix}$ ... $\begin{bmatrix} \text{INDEX} & \boxed{1} \end{bmatrix}$

Following standard mathematical practice, however, we will continue to use multiple occurrences of a given index to indicate that two features have the same index as their value.

(32)

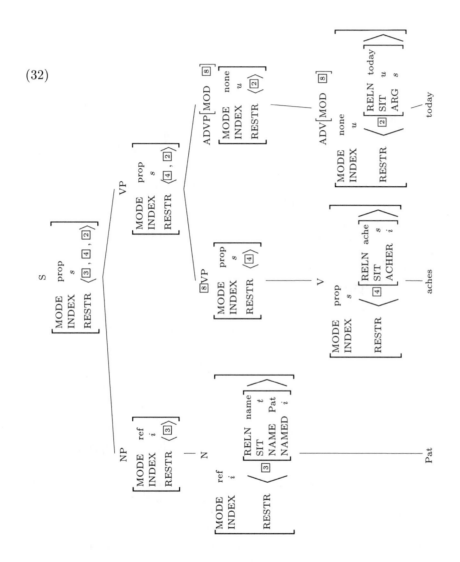

In the previous chapter, we wrote this rule as follows:

(33) $\boxed{1}$ → $\boxed{1}^+$ CONJ $\boxed{1}$

This is equivalent to the following formulation, where the Kleene plus has been replaced by a schematic enumeration of the conjunct daughters:

(34) $\boxed{1}$ → $\boxed{1}_1$ ... $\boxed{1}_{n-1}$ CONJ $\boxed{1}_n$

We will employ this notation for now because it lets us enumerate schematically the arguments that the semantic analysis of conjunctions requires.

Unlike the other relations we have used for semantic analysis, where each predication specifies a fixed (and small) number of roles, the relations that express the meanings of conjunctions like *and* and *or* allow any number of arguments. Thus each conjunct of coordinate structures like the following is a semantic argument of the conjunction:

(35) a. Chris [[walks]₁, [eats broccoli]₂, and [plays squash]₃].
      b. [[Chris walks]₁, [Pat eats broccoli]₂, and [Sandy plays squash]₃].

Because the number of arguments is not fixed, the predications for conjunctions allow not just indices as arguments, but lists of indices. Consequently, the sentences in (35) may be represented in terms of a semantic structure like the following:

(36)
$$
\begin{bmatrix}
\text{MODE} & \text{prop} \\
\text{INDEX} & s \\
\text{RESTR} & \left\langle
\begin{bmatrix}
\text{RELN} & \text{and} \\
\text{SIT} & s \\
\text{ARGS} & \langle t,u,v \rangle
\end{bmatrix},
\begin{bmatrix}
\text{RELN} & \text{walk} \\
\text{SIT} & t \\
& ...
\end{bmatrix},
\right. \\
\qquad
\left.
\begin{bmatrix}
\text{RELN} & \text{eat} \\
\text{SIT} & u \\
& ...
\end{bmatrix},
\begin{bmatrix}
\text{RELN} & \text{play} \\
\text{SIT} & v \\
& ...
\end{bmatrix}
\right\rangle
\end{bmatrix}
$$

Note that it is the conjunction's index ('s' in (36)) that is the index of the entire coordinate phrase. Otherwise, the work of combining the RESTR values of all the daughters in a coordinate structure to form the RESTR value of the mother is taken care of by the Semantic Compositionality Principle.

Let us assume then that the lexical entry for a conjunction looks roughly as shown in (37). The Coordination Rule must then be modified to identify the indices of the conjuncts with the ARGS value of the conjunction.

(37)

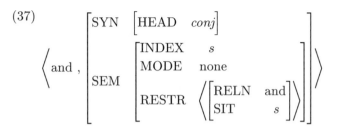

$$\left\langle \text{and} , \begin{bmatrix} \text{SYN} & \begin{bmatrix} \text{HEAD} & conj \end{bmatrix} \\ \text{SEM} & \begin{bmatrix} \text{INDEX} & s \\ \text{MODE} & \text{none} \\ \text{RESTR} & \left\langle \begin{bmatrix} \text{RELN} & and \\ \text{SIT} & s \end{bmatrix} \right\rangle \end{bmatrix} \end{bmatrix} \right\rangle$$

Before doing this, however, we must consider the syntactic matching of the conjuncts. In our earlier formulation, we identified the entire grammatical category of all conjuncts (and their mother). But, as we have just seen, the semantics of conjuncts is not shared. (In fact, it would be pragmatically quite strange to conjoin multiple expressions that mean the same thing). Rather, the conjuncts become semantic arguments of the conjunction, and the combined list of predications must become the RESTR value of the mother of the coordinate structure. Given the need to treat the semantics separately, a reasonable hypothesis about the sharing in a coordinate structure is that the SYNTAX value of all conjuncts and of their mother is the same. This leads us to the following reformulation of our Coordination Rule:[13]

(38) Coordination Rule

$$\begin{bmatrix} \text{SYN} & \boxed{0} \\ \text{IND} & s_0 \end{bmatrix} \rightarrow$$

$$\begin{bmatrix} \text{SYN} & \boxed{0} \\ \text{IND} & s_1 \end{bmatrix} \cdots \begin{bmatrix} \text{SYN} & \boxed{0} \\ \text{IND} & s_{n-1} \end{bmatrix} \begin{bmatrix} \text{HEAD} & conj \\ \text{IND} & s_0 \\ \text{RESTR} & \left\langle \begin{bmatrix} \text{ARGS} & \langle s_1 \dots s_n \rangle \end{bmatrix} \right\rangle \end{bmatrix} \begin{bmatrix} \text{SYN} & \boxed{0} \\ \text{IND} & s_n \end{bmatrix}$$

This rule accomplishes a number of goals, including

- requiring that all conjuncts of a coordinate structure have identical values for HEAD, SPR, and COMPS,
- collecting the RESTR values of all daughters into the RESTR list of the mother (guaranteed because the structures built in accordance with this rule must satisfy the Semantic Compositionality Principle),

---

[13]The careful reader will note that we have omitted the feature name 'SEM' to the left of 'IND' in each of the terms of (38). In the remainder of the book, we will often simplify our feature structure descriptions in this way, leaving out some of the outer layers of feature names when the information of interest is embedded within the feature structure description. We will only simplify in this way when no ambiguity about our intended meaning can result.

- identifying the indices of the conjuncts with the semantic arguments of the conjunction, and
- identifying the index of the conjunction with that of the coordinate structure.

These effects are illustrated in the following SD, which describes a (coordinate) phrase structure satisfying the Coordination Rule.

(39)

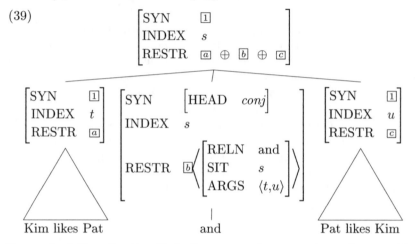

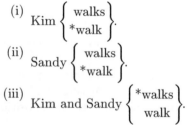

| Kim likes Pat | and | Pat likes Kim |

Our revised Coordination Rule thus goes a long way toward accounting for sentences containing coordinate structures and associating them with appropriate meanings.

Problem 1: NP Coordination

Consider the following data.

(i) Kim $\left\{ \begin{array}{l} \text{walks} \\ \text{*walk} \end{array} \right\}$.

(ii) Sandy $\left\{ \begin{array}{l} \text{walks} \\ \text{*walk} \end{array} \right\}$.

(iii) Kim and Sandy $\left\{ \begin{array}{l} \text{*walks} \\ \text{walk} \end{array} \right\}$.

A. What conclusion can you draw about the NUMBER value of coordinate NPs?

Now consider the question of what the PERSON value of coordinate NPs is. Choice of verb form does not usually help very much in determining the person of the subject, because those whose

AGR value is *non-3sing* are compatible with a subject of any person (except those whose AGR is *3sing*).

However, there is another way to detect the person of the subject NP. If the VP contains a direct object reflexive pronoun, then (as we saw in Chapter 1) the reflexive must agree in person and number with the subject. This co-occurrence pattern is shown by the following examples.

(iv) $\left\{\begin{array}{l} \text{You} \\ \text{*I} \\ \text{*She} \\ \text{*They} \\ \text{*We} \end{array}\right\}$ distinguished yourself. (2nd person singular)

(v) $\left\{\begin{array}{l} \text{She} \\ \text{*You} \\ \text{*I} \\ \text{*They} \\ \text{*We} \end{array}\right\}$ distinguished herself. (3rd person singular)

(vi) $\left\{\begin{array}{l} \text{We} \\ \text{*You} \\ \text{*I} \\ \text{*They} \\ \text{*She} \end{array}\right\}$ distinguished ourselves. (1st person plural)

(vii) $\left\{\begin{array}{l} \text{They} \\ \text{*We} \\ \text{*You} \\ \text{*I} \\ \text{*She} \end{array}\right\}$ distinguished themselves. (3rd person plural)

In light of this patterning, we can now consider the person of coordinate NPs by examining examples like the following:

(viii) You and she distinguished $\left\{\begin{array}{l} \text{yourselves} \\ \text{*themselves} \\ \text{*ourselves} \end{array}\right\}$.

(ix) You and I distinguished $\left\{\begin{array}{l} \text{*yourselves} \\ \text{*themselves} \\ \text{ourselves} \end{array}\right\}$.

B. Construct further examples of sentences with coordinate subjects (stick to the conjunction *and*) that could help you discover what the person value of the coordinate NP is for every combination of PERSON value on the conjuncts. State the principles for determining the PERSON value of a coordinate NP in as general terms as you can.

C. Our Coordination Rule in (38) cannot easily be weakened to allow conjuncts to have disparate HEAD values. Otherwise we would run the risk of generating examples like the following:

(x) *Kim [walks] and [happy].
(xi) *Pat visited [Chris and sad].

So on the basis of your results in (A) and (B), what conclusion should you draw about the analysis of NP coordination?

⚠ **Problem 2: Modes of Coordination**
Consider the following data.

(i)   Kim left and Sandy left.
(ii)   ?*Kim left and did Sandy leave.
(iii) ?*Did Sandy leave and Kim left.
(iv)   Did Sandy leave and did Kim leave?
(v)   Go away and leave me alone!
(vi)   ?*Kim left and leave me alone!
(vii) ?*Leave me alone and Kim left.
(viii) ?*Leave me alone and did Kim leave?
(ix)   ?*Did Kim leave and leave me alone!

A Formulate a generalization about the MODE value of conjuncts (and their mother) that could account for these data.

B Modify the Coordination Rule in (38) so that it enforces the generalization you formulated in (A).

5.8 Summary

In this chapter, we introduced fundamental issues in the study of linguistic meaning and extended our grammar to include semantic descriptions. We then provided a systematic account of the relation between syntactic structure and semantic interpretation based on two constraints: the Semantic Compositionality Principle and the Semantic Inheritance Principle. These principles together provide a general account of how the semantics of a phrase is related to the semantics of its daughters. This chapter also presented a rudimentary analysis of modification and extended the treatment of coordinate structures to include an account of their linguistic meaning.

5.9 Further Reading

Essentially all work on linguistic pragmatics builds directly on the pioneering work of the philosopher H. Paul Grice (see Grice 1989). A seminal work in modern research on natural language semantics is Frege's (1892) essay, 'Über Sinn und Bedeutung' (usually translated as 'On Sense and Reference'), which has been translated and reprinted in many anthologies (e.g. Geach and Black, eds., (1980)). More recently, the papers of Richard Montague (Montague, 1970) had a revolutionary influence, but they are extremely technical and difficult. An elementary presentation of his theory is given by Dowty, Wall, and Peters (1981). General introductory texts in semantics include Chierchia and McConnell-Ginet (1990), Gamut (1991), and de Swart (1998). Shorter overviews of semantics include Bach (1989), Barwise and Etchemendy (1989), and Partee (1995).

6

How the Grammar Works

6.1 A Factorization of Grammatical Information

Four chapters ago, we began modifying the formalism of context-free grammar to better adapt it to the sorts of generalizations we find in natural languages. We broke grammatical categories down into features, and then we broke the values of features down into features, as well. In the process, we moved more and more syntactic information out of the grammar rules and into the lexicon. In effect, we changed our theory of grammar so that the rules give only very general patterns that cut across grammatical categories. Details about which expressions can go with which are specified in lexical entries in terms of valence features.

With the expanded ability of our new feature structure complexes to express cross-categorial generalizations, our four remaining grammar rules cover a wide range of cases. Two of them – the rules introducing complements and specifiers – were discussed extensively in Chapter 4. The third one – a generalization of our old rules introducing PP modifiers to VP and NOM – was illustrated in the previous chapter. The fourth is the coordination schema. The formal statements of these rules are given in (1), along with informal translations (given in italics below the rules).[1]

(1) **Head-Complement Rule**

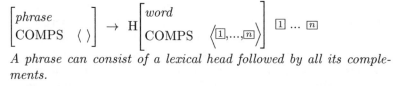

A phrase can consist of a lexical head followed by all its complements.

---

[1] It should be noted that the Head-Modifier Rule does not cover all kinds of modifiers. In particular, some modifiers – such as adjectives inside NPs – precede the heads that they modify. To accommodate such modifiers, we would need an additional grammar rule.

Head-Specifier Rule

$$\begin{bmatrix} phrase \\ \text{SPR} \quad \langle \ \rangle \end{bmatrix} \rightarrow \boxed{1} \quad \text{H} \begin{bmatrix} phrase \\ \text{SPR} \quad \langle \boxed{1} \rangle \end{bmatrix}$$

A phrase can consist of a phrasal head preceded by its specifier.

Head-Modifier Rule

$$[phrase] \rightarrow \text{H}\boxed{1}[phrase] \quad \begin{bmatrix} phrase \\ \text{MOD} \quad \boxed{1} \end{bmatrix}$$

A phrase can consist of a phrasal head followed by a compatible modifier phrase.

Coordination Rule

$$\begin{bmatrix} \text{SYN} \quad \boxed{0} \\ \text{IND} \quad s_0 \end{bmatrix} \rightarrow$$

$$\begin{bmatrix} \text{SYN} \ \boxed{0} \\ \text{IND} \ s_1 \end{bmatrix} \cdots \begin{bmatrix} \text{SYN} \ \boxed{0} \\ \text{IND} \ s_{n-1} \end{bmatrix} \begin{bmatrix} \text{HEAD} \quad conj \\ \text{IND} \quad s_0 \\ \text{RESTR} \ \left\langle \begin{bmatrix} \text{ARGS} \ \langle s_1 \ldots s_n \rangle \end{bmatrix} \right\rangle \end{bmatrix} \begin{bmatrix} \text{SYN} \ \boxed{0} \\ \text{IND} \ s_n \end{bmatrix}$$

Any number of occurrences of elements of the same syntactic category can be conjoined to make a coordinate element of that category.

In addition to our grammar rules, we must provide (as we did in the case of CFGs) some characterization of the 'initial symbols', corresponding to the types of phrases that can stand alone as sentences of the language. We postpone a characterization of this until Chapter 9, when we will have introduced a method for distinguishing finite (that is, tensed) clauses from others.

The richer feature structures we are now using, together with our highly schematized rules, have required us to refine our notion of how a grammar is related to the fully determinate phrase structures of the language and to the informal descriptions of those structures that we will use to explicate those structures. Intuitively, here is how it works: First, each lexical entry licenses a family of word structures – each of which is a nonbranching tree whose mother is a resolved feature structure satisfying the feature structure description of the lexical entry.

Put somewhat differently, given a lexical entry $\langle \omega, \Phi \rangle$, each of these word structures must satisfy the following lexical SD:

(2)　　　　Φ
　　　　　　$|$
　　　　　　ω

Such lexical SDs form the bottom layer of well-formed phrasal SDs. They can be combined[2] into larger SDs in the ways permitted by the grammar rules, filling in features as required by our four principles: the Semantic Compositionality Principle, the Head Feature Principle, the Valence Principle, and the Semantic Inheritance Principle. This process can apply to its own output, making ever larger phrasal SDs. So long as each local SD that we construct is licensed by a grammar rule and conforms to these principles, it is well formed. Typically, each node in a well-formed SD will contain some information that was stipulated by a rule and other information that percolated up (metaphorically speaking) from lower nodes (and ultimately from the lexical entries) via the principles.

For most of the material presented in the chapters that follow, an intuitive grasp of how the lexicon, grammar rules, and principles interact to license phrasal SDs will suffice. Nevertheless, for completeness we include an explicit definition of the resolved structures permitted by our grammar as an appendix to this chapter. Our SDs contain exactly as much information as is obtained by unifying the constraints that percolated up from the daughters, the constraints that are specified in each rule, and those constraints that are part of our general theory (the Head Feature Principle, etc.). Hence the relation between our phrasal SDs and the phrase structures that satisfy them should be transparent: a phrasal SD consolidates all relevant conditions that a given phrase structure must satisfy.

We have formulated our theory so that, as successively larger SDs are produced, the descriptions of the (nonterminal) nodes expand through unification. That is, information that is left underspecified in an SD often needs to be included if it is to be embedded in a larger SD. This important side effect of unifying SDs can be illustrated simply. Consider the SD in (3).

---

[2]Our informal discussion is worded in terms of a process of building trees up from the bottom. This is a conceptually natural way of thinking about it, but it should not be taken too literally. The formal definition of well-formed tree structure that we give below is deliberately nonprocedural.

(3)

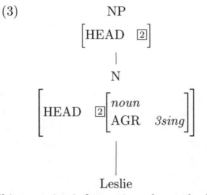

This contains information about the HEAD value of the phrase (unified with the HEAD value of the N dominating *Leslie*). But when this SD is embedded within a larger one like (4), licensed by the Head-Complement Rule, the result is as shown in (4).

(4)

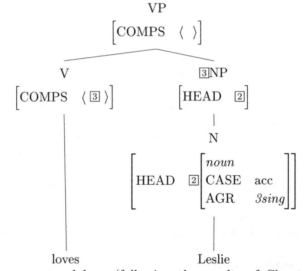

We have assumed here (following the results of Chapter 4, problem 6) that the lexical entry for *loves* specifies that its complement is [CASE acc]. Because the Head-Complement Rule identifies the head daughter's COMPS list with the list of (the feature structures of the) complement daughters, the accusative case specification is part of the

SD of the object NP's HEAD value. And since that NP's HEAD specification is identified with the HEAD specification of its head daughter (namely, the N dominating *Leslie*), it follows that the accusative case specification is part of the SD of this embedded category as well.

The information specified by our rules and lexical entries is thus partial information. Each rule says, in effect, that subtrees of a certain kind are sanctioned, but the rule only specifies some of the constraints that the SDs that it licenses must obey. Likewise, a lexical entry says that certain trees dominating the phonological form in that entry are sanctioned, but the entry only specifies some of the information relevant at higher levels of structure. The general principles of our theory constrain the ways in which feature values can be distributed in well-formed phrase structure trees. The unification of partial descriptions (or constraints) is the basic method that allows the job of determining well-formedness to be distributed among the pieces of our grammatical system in a parsimonious way.

In short, we have arrived at a particular factorization of the information necessary for a precise account of grammatical descriptions. By far the richest source of information in this factorization is the lexicon. That is, our account embodies the claim that both the problem of determining which strings of words constitute well-formed sentences and the problem of specifying the linguistic meaning of sentences depend mostly on the nature of words. Of course, it must also be recognized that there are many regularities about which words go together (and how they go together). The theoretical constructs summarized here capture a number of such regularities; subsequent chapters will provide ways of capturing more.

6.2 A Detailed Example

The components of our grammatical theory interact so as to license certain phrase structure trees as well-formed sentences, but not others. The nature of these interactions can best be understood through careful analysis of linguistic examples. In this subsection, we show in detail how the grammar of English, as we have developed it to this point, would handle one simple sentence of English, namely:

(5) They sent us a letter.

We begin our analysis with the lexical SD for the word *letter*.

(6)

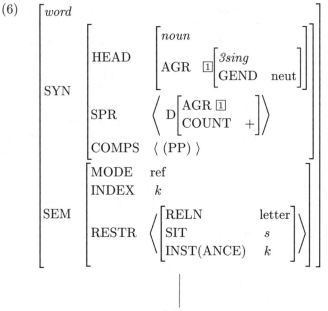

letter

This combines with zero complements via the Head-Complement Rule to give the SD shown in (7). Note that the COMPS value is disambiguated (to the empty list) by the presence of no complements in this SD. The Head Feature Principle (HFP) is obeyed; the SPR specifications obey the Valence Principle; and the COMPS specifications are as dictated by the Head-Complement Rule.

The lexical SD for the word *a* is (8). Providing semantics for determiners (such as quantifiers) is something we have avoided, since it would take us too far afield. So we simply omit any description of the determiner's SEM value.

(7)

$$\begin{bmatrix} phrase \\ \text{SYN} \begin{bmatrix} \text{HEAD} & \boxed{27} \\ \text{SPR} & \langle \boxed{28} \rangle \\ \text{COMPS} & \langle\,\rangle \end{bmatrix} \\ \text{SEM} \begin{bmatrix} \text{MODE} & ref \\ \text{INDEX} & k \\ \text{RESTR} & \boxed{a} \end{bmatrix} \end{bmatrix}$$

|

$$\begin{bmatrix} word \\ \text{SYN} \begin{bmatrix} \text{HEAD} & \boxed{27}\begin{bmatrix} noun \\ \text{AGR} & \boxed{1}\begin{bmatrix} 3sing \\ \text{GEND} & neut \end{bmatrix} \end{bmatrix} \\ \text{SPR} & \langle \boxed{28}\text{D}[\text{AGR}\ \boxed{1}] \rangle \\ \text{COMPS} & \langle\,\rangle \end{bmatrix} \\ \text{SEM} \begin{bmatrix} \text{MODE} & ref \\ \text{INDEX} & k \\ \text{RESTR} & \boxed{a}\left\langle \begin{bmatrix} \text{RELN} & letter \\ \text{SIT} & s \\ \text{INST} & k \end{bmatrix} \right\rangle \end{bmatrix} \end{bmatrix}$$

|

letter

(8)

$$\begin{bmatrix} word \\ \text{SYN} \begin{bmatrix} \text{HEAD} \begin{bmatrix} det \\ \text{COUNT} & + \\ \text{AGR} & [3sing] \end{bmatrix} \end{bmatrix} \end{bmatrix}$$

|

a

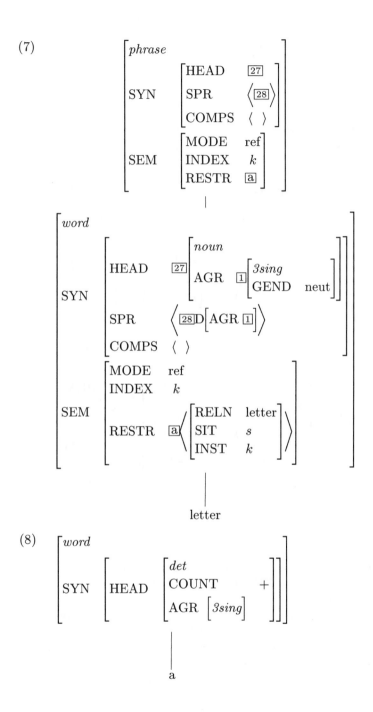

The following SD results from combining (7) and (8) via the Head-Specifier Rule:

(9)

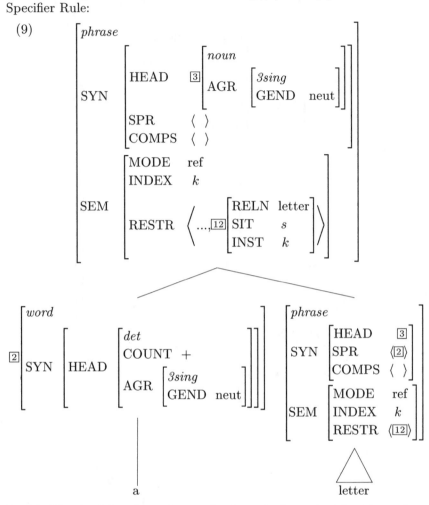

In this SD, the left subtree is exactly the one shown in (8), except that the feature specification [GEND neut] has been added, via unification with the SPR value of the head noun. This unification is required by the Head-Specifier Rule, which licenses the combination of this determiner with this noun. The right subtree in (9) is exactly the one shown in (7) (though abbreviated with a triangle). (9) also obeys the HFP: the HEAD value of the head daughter is identified with that of the mother. And it obeys the Valence Principle: the COMPS value of the phrase is the same as that of the head daughter (the empty list). The mother's SPR value is the empty list, as required by the Head-Specifier Rule.

The Semantic Inheritance Principle says that the MODE and INDEX values of the head daughter must be shared by the mother, which is the case in (9). And the Semantic Compositionality Principle requires that the mother's RESTR value be the sum of the two daughters' RESTR lists. Since we waved our hands at the semantics of *a*, we do not have all the information needed to specify the RESTR value of the whole NP. To indicate this, we have written '...' for the contribution to the RESTR of the NP made by *a*.

The lexical entry for the pronoun *us* is quite straightforward, except for the RESTR list in the semantics. In the following, we have chosen to characterize the meaning of *us* roughly as reference to a group of which the speaker is a member. We have formalized this as a RESTR list with components, but there are many other possible ways of doing this. Our version gives rise to the following lexical SD:

(10)
$$
\begin{bmatrix}
word \\
\text{SYN} \begin{bmatrix}
\text{HEAD} \begin{bmatrix} noun \\ \text{CASE} \quad acc \\ \text{AGR} \begin{bmatrix} non\text{-}3sing \\ \text{PER} \quad 1st \\ \text{NUM} \quad pl \end{bmatrix} \end{bmatrix} \\
\text{SPR} \quad \langle \; \rangle \\
\text{COMPS} \quad \langle \; \rangle
\end{bmatrix} \\
\text{SEM} \begin{bmatrix}
\text{MODE} \quad ref \\
\text{INDEX} \quad j \\
\text{RESTR} \left\langle \begin{bmatrix} \text{RELN} \quad group \\ \text{SIT} \quad t \\ \text{INST} \quad j \end{bmatrix}, \begin{bmatrix} \text{RELN} \quad speaker \\ \text{SIT} \quad u \\ \text{INST} \quad l \end{bmatrix}, \begin{bmatrix} \text{RELN} \quad member \\ \text{SIT} \quad v \\ \text{SET} \quad j \\ \text{ELEMENT} \quad l \end{bmatrix} \right\rangle
\end{bmatrix}
\end{bmatrix}
$$

|
us

past-vb (the type), 364
pdp-lxm (the type), 181, 203, 205, 386, 387
PER(SON), 61, 88, 122, 124, 153
perfective, 441
perfective *have*
  noniterability of, 302
performance, 218, 222, 231, 441
person, 68, 88, 90, 164, 227, 442
persuade, 288, 290, 292
philosophy, 13
PHON(OLOGY), 357, 358, 363, 370, 372, 374
phonetics, 323, 328, 442
phonology, 3, 190, 323, 420, 442
  phonological description, 49
  phonological form, 131
  phonological information, 383
phrasal category, 29, 36, 41
phrasal construction, 359
phrasal satisfaction, 145, 213, 229, 230, 355, 370, 377, 402
phrasal SD, 67, 71, 129, 137
phrasal sign, 369–382
phrase, 29, 35, 38, 49, 62, 75, 128, 355, 358, 369, 370, 374, 377, 415, 420
phrase (the type), 55, 56, 203, 204, 372, 380, 386, 387
phrase hierarchies, 421
phrase structure, 63, 65, 128, 131, 383, 412, 418, 421, 422
  grammar, 422
  model, 65
  phrase type, 383
  rule (PS rule), 30, 34, 37, 45, 55, 56, 58–59, 62, 70, 72, 74, 75, 84–85, 96, 99–100, 114, 127–128, 211, 264, 326, 401, 415
pia-lxm (the type), 361
picture-nouns, 177
pitch accent, 383
piv-lxm (the type), 180, 203, 205, 361, 389

plans and goals, 103
plural, 20, 43, 64, 90, 92, 153, 178
  form, 187
  noun, 101, 187
  pronoun, 153, 186, 187
  verb, 88
Plural Noun Lexical Rule, 186, 187, 215, 405
pn-lxm (the type), 176, 177, 203, 204, 357, 386, 388, 392
P-OBJ, 156–160, 182, 236, 248
POS, 55–57, 60, 61
pos (the type), 183, 203, 206, 227, 386, 390
possessive, 35, 141, 442
  's, 141
  pronouns, 142
PP, *see* prepositional phrase
PP attachment ambiguities, 227
PP[by], 236
PP complement, 180, 182
  optional, 82
PP modifier, 58, 85, 127
pragmatic inference, 16–17, 103, 104
pragmatic plausibility, 160
pragmatics, 17, 102–104, 121, 226, 383, 421, 442
PRED, 252
pred (the type), 109, 203, 386
predication, 108–110, 112, 113, 120, 121, 179, 195, 278
predication (the type), 109, 207, 391
predicative, 158, 252
  complement, 255
  nominal, 252
  phrase, 298
prediction, 315
prefix, 194
prep (the type), 61, 203, 206, 386, 390
prep-arg-lxm (the type), 361
prep-lxm (the type), 182, 183, 203, 205, 386, 387

Name Index